Lecture Notes in Computer Science   6995

Commenced Publication in 1973
Founding and Former Series Editors:
Gerhard Goos, Juris Hartmanis, and J

T0092450

Editorial Board

Johanne Cohen   Patrick Maillé
Burkhard Stiller (Eds.)

Economics of Converged, Internet-Based Networks

7th International Workshop on Internet Charging
and QoS Technologies, ICQT 2011
Paris, France, October 24, 2011
Proceedings

 Springer

Volume Editors

Johanne Cohen
Université de Versailles Saint-Quentin-en-Yvelines
Laboratoire d'Informatique PRiSM
45, Avenue des États-Unis, 78035 Versailles Cedex, France
E-mail: johanne.cohen@prism.uvsq.fr

Patrick Maillé
Institut Télécom/Télécom Bretagne
Networks, Security, Multimedia Department
2, Rue de la Châtaigneraie, 35576 Cesson-Sévigné Cedex, France
E-mail: patrick.maille@telecom-bretagne.eu

Burkhard Stiller
University of Zurich
Department of Informatics IFI
Binzmühlestrasse 14, 8050 Zürich, Switzerland
E-mail: stiller@ifi.uzh.ch

ISSN 0302-9743   e-ISSN 1611-3349
ISBN 978-3-642-24546-6   e-ISBN 978-3-642-24547-3
DOI 10.1007/978-3-642-24547-3
Springer Heidelberg Dordrecht London New York

Library of Congress Control Number: 2011937950

CR Subject Classification (1998): C.2, H.4, H.3, J.1, K.4.4, K.6.4, I.2

LNCS Sublibrary: SL 5 – Computer Communication Networks and Telecommunications

Typesetting: Camera-ready by author, data conversion by Scientific Publishing Services, Chennai, India

Printed on acid-free paper

Springer is part of Springer Science+Business Media (www.springer.com)

Preface

With the appearance of new technologies and new services, the nature of the economic stakes in the ICT (Information and Communication Technologies) sector is continually evolving. An illustration is the soaring number of providers, who base their business models on publicity instead of bandwidth selling. Following the same trends, the power relationships have radically changed in the last decade, between the providers offering connectivity, and those managing services and user identities (content provid- ers, cloud computing providers, social networks).

Therefore, the 7th International Workshop on Internet Charging and QoS Technology (ICQT 2011) is devoted to discussing the most recent approaches, models, and mechanisms in the highly important research area of network economics. The present volume of the Lecture Notes in Computer Science series includes those papers presented at ICQT 2011 — collocated this year with the 7th International Conference on Network and Service Management — taking place on October 24, 2011, in Paris, France and hosted by the Paris Descartes University.

For the success of future QoS-enabled communication services, the emergence of viable regulation policies, business models, pricing schemes, and charging and accounting mechanisms is of paramount importance. In particular, the possibility of providing service guarantees, the efficiency of pricing mechanisms, and the economics of inter-domain services are of utmost urgency. Thus, they determine — in the form of three technical sessions — the core of the ICQT 2011 program. All contributions included in this volume fit perfectly into the general scope of the international ICQT workshop series, which is mainly characterized by the focus on identifying novel service charging solutions, investigating and evaluating their technical feasibility, and consolidating technical and economic mechanisms for enabling a fast, guaranteed, and efficient charging of services. This is of fundamental importance for the future evolution of Internet-based networks.

This year's ICQT followed the already established tradition of a vivid workshop series on charging and QoS technology issues, which started back in 2001 with the first ICQT workshop in the framework of the Annual Meeting of the German Society for Computer Science (GI) and the Austrian Computer Society 2001 in Vienna, Austria. In 2002, ICQT was collocated with the QofIS 2002 workshop in Zürich, Switzerland, in 2003 with the NGC 2003 workshop in Munich, Germany, and in 2004 again with QofIS 2004 in Barcelona, Spain. In 2006, ICQT was hosted by the University Institute of Technology (IUT), St. Malo, France together with ACM SIGMETRICS 2006, and in 2009 by the Rheinisch-Westfälische Technische Hochschule (RWTH) in Aachen, Germany, together with the IFIP Networking 2009.

As in the past, ICQT 2011 brought together researchers from the areas of technology and economics in both industry and academia to discuss key improvements and to support further economics in these fields. The combination of micro-economic models, auctions, game theory (cooperative and non-cooperative), peer-provided services, and regulation policies addressed important aspects at the intersection of networking research and business modeling. Thus, ICQT 2011 provided a truly interdisciplinary forum for analyzing topics at the overlap of those areas. Like all of its predecessors, ICQT 2011 consisted of a single-track one-day event, which has proved to be especially suitable for stimulating the interaction between and the active participation of the workshop audience.

In summary, the workshop started with a keynote presentation delivered by Andrew Odlyzko, who is internationally recognized to be one of the most distinguished research fellows in the area. The following three technical sessions included a total of six full papers, which were selected after a thorough review process out of a total number of 18 submissions. The resulting final program demonstrated again the international scope of this workshop series and included papers from Europe, Asia, North America, and South America. The international orientation of ICQT is also reflected in the composition of its Technical Program Committee, whose members again devoted their excellent knowledge together with many hours of their precious time to provide the basis for a highly qualified technical program and, thus, to contribute in an unfailing way to the technical and research success of ICQT.

Furthermore, the editors would like to express their thanks to Patrick Zwickl, the ICQT 2011 webmaster for his excellent work. Special thanks go to the organizers of the CNSM 2011 conference for enabling the collocation of ICQT 2011 with their renowned event, as well as to the local organizers. Finally, all three editors would like to address their thanks to Springer, and especially Anna Kramer, for a very smooth cooperation on finalizing these proceedings. Additionally, special thanks go to the support of the European COST Action IS0605 "Econ@Tel" and their Working Group WG4 researchers.

October 2011

Johanne Cohen
Patrick Maillé
Burkhard Stiller

Organization

Program TPC Co-chairs ICQT 2011

Johanne Cohen   University of Versailles, France
Patrick Maillé   Institut Télécom/Télécom Bretagne, France

Steering Committee

Peter Reichl   FTW Vienna, Austria
Burkhard Stiller   University of Zürich, Switzerland
Bruno Tuffin   INRIA Rennes Bretagne-Atlantique, France

Publications Chair

Burkhard Stiller   University of Zürich, Switzerland

Technical Program Committee ICQT 2011

Jörn Altmann   Seoul National University, Korea
Dominique Barth   University of Versailles, France
Manos Dramitinos   Athens University of Economics and Business, Greece
Loubna Echabbi   INPT, Morocco
Ivan Gojmerac   FTW Vienna, Austria
José Luis Gómez Barroso   UNED, Spain
Heikki Hämmäinen   Aalto University, Finland
Maurizio Naldi   University of Rome Tor Vergata, Italy
Andrew Odlyzko   University of Minnesota, USA
Ariel Orda   Technion, Israel
Fernando Paganini   Universidad ORT, Uruguay
Hélia Pouyllau   Alcatel-Lucent Bell Labs, France
David Reeves   North Carolina State University, USA
Günter Schäfer   University of Ilmenau, Germany
Nicolas Stier   Columbia University, USA
Corinne Touati   INRIA, France
Tuan Trinh Anh   BME Budapest, Hungary
Jean Walrand   University of California, Berkeley, USA

Reviewers

A set of very detailed and constructive reviews for papers submitted to ICQT
2011 were provided by all ICQT reviewers, corresponding to the full Program
Committee members as stated above, and additionally: Ashraf Bany Mohammed,
Olivier Bournez, René Golembewski, Michael Grey, László Gyarmati, Emmanuel
Hyon, Vijay Kamble, Sam- son Lasaulce, Peter Reichl, and Sander Wozniak.
Therefore, it is with great pleasure that the Program Co-chairs thank all those
reviewers for their important work.

Table of Contents

Economics, QoS, and Charging
in the Next Great Telecom Revolution

Andrew Odlyzko

University of Minnesota, USA
odlyzko@umn.edu

Abstract. While the Internet has attracted the bulk of the attention from the public as well as from researchers, the growth of wireless has had a far larger impact on the world, as measured by the number of users, the revenues, or the profits. Technology is leading to a convergence of the two areas, and this will be the next great telecom revolution. The relation between technological progress and consumer demand differs greatly in wireless from what continues to prevail on the wireline Internet, and this is leading to a reconsideration of some of the QoS and charging schemes that failed to find acceptance in the past. A perspective will be presented on what approaches are most likely to succeed, and why.

J. Cohen, P. Maillé, and B. Stiller (Eds.): ICQT 2011, LNCS 6995, p. 1, 2011.
© Springer-Verlag Berlin Heidelberg 2011

Compensation Policies and Risk in Service Level Agreements: A Value-at-Risk Approach under the ON-OFF Service Model

Loretta Mastroeni[1] and Maurizio Naldi[2]

[1] Università di Roma Tre, Dipartimento di Economia, Via Silvio D'Amico, 00145
Roma, Italy
mastroen@uniroma3.it
[2] Università di Roma *Tor Vergata*, Dipartimento di Informatica, Sistemi e
Produzione, Via del Politecnico 1, 00133 Roma, Italy
naldi@disp.uniroma2.it

Abstract. Service Level Agreements define the obligations of service
providers towards their customers. One of such obligations is the compensation that customers receive in the case of service degradation or
interruption. This obligation exposes the service provider to the risk of
paying large amounts of money in the case of massive disruptions. The
evaluation of such risk is preliminary to any countermeasure the service
provider may wish to take to mitigate the risk. In this paper we evaluate
the probability distribution of economical losses associated to service failures under a Markovian ON-OFF service model. We provide expressions
for such distributions under three compensation policies, linked respectively to the number of failures, the number of outages lasting more
than a prescribed threshold, and the cumulative downtime over a finite
time horizon. In order to provide a single measure of risk, we compute
the Value-at-Risk (VaR) for those compensation policies. We show that
the VaR provides an accurate view of the risk incurred by the service
provider, and allows to differentiate compensation policies, even when
they lead to equal average losses.

Keywords: Service Level Agreement, Risk theory, Compensation policies.

1 Introduction

In the contract between a service provider and a customer, Service Level Agreements (SLA) define the level of service that the former commits to provide to
the latter. That commitment is a contractual obligation, which includes, or at
least should include, a set of performance bounds, amenable to being measured.
If the performance bounds are not met, the SLA (hence, the contract) is vi-
olated. The SLA may include a compensation mechanism, which defines how
the service provider is to compensate the customer for SLA violations. Even if
the SLA doesn't contemplate a compensation mechanism, the definition of the
service level entitles the customer to ask for compensation.

J. Cohen, P. Maillé, and B. Stiller (Eds.): ICQT 2011, LNCS 6995, pp. 2–13, 2011.

In any case, the presence of a SLA exposes the service provider to the risk of monetary losses due to the violation of SLA obligations. The losses incurred depend both on the definition of the compensation policy and on the frequency and extent of the violations. But they are a random quantity, since they depend on the occurrence of those events that lead to a SLA violation. Examples of such events are the accidental cut of a fiber link, the sudden failure of a network device, the destruction a network facility by a fire.

The compensations erode the profit made by the service provider, and may significantly alter its economic status. A lot of attention has been paid to the technical means that can be employed to mitigate the risk. In particular, the design of resilient network architectures has been the focus of many research efforts [1]. Whatever the reduction of risk achieved by those means, the service provider has anyway to evaluate what level of losses it faces. It has to do it for three main reasons. The first one is that no network architecture can guarantee that no SLA violations will take place. Even with a very resilient network, the service provider incurs a nonzero residual risk, and has to assess if it is sustainable. The second reason concerns the economical effectiveness of those technical means. The improvement of network reliability (which leads to the reduction of SLA violations) is achieved through significant investments, which are accomplished to reduce the expenses associated to compensations. Those investments are justified, if they are counterbalanced by a reduction of losses of at least equal amount. But that comparison cannot be made if the service provider has not evaluated its SLA-related losses. Finally, the service provider may contemplate different compensation policies to propose to its customers. Since those policies generally lead to different losses, the service provider should select the most favourable, or that leading to the best trade-off between potential losses and customer satisfaction. Again, that selection is not possible, if it is not supported by the evaluation of the losses. But the evaluation of those losses has not received much attention in the literature, though the knowledge of the risk associated to service level can be exploited to optimize the SLA/contract conditions [2].

In this paper, we aim to fill the gap and provide a first assessment of the losses incurred by a service provider because of the compensations to be paid to customers for SLA violations. We consider a simple ON-OFF service model and three compensation policies, which cover the commonest cases. For each compensation policy, we provide the analytical expression of the probability distribution of losses. In addition, as a synthetic measure of risk, we borrow the Value-at-Risk from the field of finance, and provide numerical values for the VaR incurred under the three policies in a number of significant cases. We show that the mean loss is not enough to perform a comparative evaluation of the three policies: even when the penalties are adjusted to lead to equal average losses under different compensation policies, the Value-at-Risk may be largely different. For some sample cases, we consistently see that the policy based on the cumulative duration of outages is riskier than that based on the number of failures.

The paper is organized as follows. In Section 2 we describe the ON-OFF service model we adopt in the subsequent calculations. In Section 3 we define the three compensation policies. We derive the probability distribution of losses in Section 4, and provide a numerical evaluation of the Value-at-Risk in Section 5. Throughout the paper we refer to the losses suffered by the service provider for a single customer.

2   The Markovian ON-OFF Service Model

The Service Level Agreement caters for service interruptions suffered by customers. We limit ourselves to consider interruptions caused by equipment failures not due to intentional attacks. In this case, we can apply a host of models derived from the reliability literature. As a first approach to the subject, we consider a simple model for the service, represented by a two-state Markovian model. In this section, we describe that model, which we employ in the following to evaluate the risk embodied in the obligations defined by the SLA.

Here we limit ourselves to consider the service as either fully available or completely unavailable. We would have a more complex model, if we consider different degrees of availability of the service (for example a communication services with reduced bandwidth, or with an increased error rate). In that case, we could consider a set of degraded quality states (and have a graceful transition between those states). In most cases, however, SLA conditions are formulated through a threshold imposed on continuous quality indicators, so that the service is considered available if that threshold is not trespassed, and unavailable otherwise. For example in [3] IP availability is defined through a threshold on the Packet Loss Ratio. Another example is the declaration of unavailability when 5 minutes have passed without a successful ping [4]; or the service can be considered to be available when 95% of the web response time samples is less than 2 seconds over a 2 hour period [4].

If we limit ourselves to the two-state model, we can consider the simple continuous-time Markovian process shown in Fig. 1, where λ and μ are the rates for ON→OFF and OFF→ON transitions respectively. The well known practical reliability measures, the Mean Time To Failure (MTTF) and Mean Time To Repair (MTTR), can be expressed as the inverses of those transition rates:

$$\begin{aligned} \text{MTTF} &= 1/\lambda \\ \text{MTTR} &= 1/\mu \end{aligned} \tag{1}$$

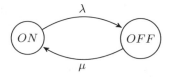

Fig. 1. Markov process model of the service state

If we consider the Markov process depicted in Fig. 1, the service undergoes a sequence of alternating availability and unavailability states. We indicate the periods of availability by the sequence $\{A_1, A_2, \ldots\}$ and those of unavailability by the sequence $\{B_1, B_2, \ldots\}$.

3   Compensation Policies

The service provider's risk depends to a large extent on its compensation policy in the case of failures, because the compensation policy determines how much is to be paid to the customer for the failures affecting it. Risk can be quantified if the compensation policy is known. In this section we first provide a general definition of compensation policy, and then describe three examples of common compensation policies, respectively determined by the number of failures, the number of long outages, and the cumulative duration of outages.

3.1   Definition

A compensation policy tells what the service provider is to pay its customer when the service fails. We assume that the compensation itself covers failures occurring over a period of time of extension T, rather than being paid on the occurrence of each failure. That assumption is reasonable since SLAs typically employ that time windowing: over each period (say, each month), the failure events that happened during that period are examined, and the compensation is computed.

In order to define the failures taking place over a generic period of duration T (without loss of generality we can consider the period $(0, T]$), we employ the variable $N \in \mathbb{N}_0$ to indicate the number of failures taking place in the period $(0 - T]$ (we have $N = 0$ when the service works uninterruptedly during that period). Each failure brings the service down for a nonzero time (the time needed to restore the service), and we can collect the duration of those downtimes in the set $\Omega = \{B_0, B_1, B_2, \ldots, B_N\}$. For sake of simplicity, we don't append a subscript to the set Ω, though its cardinality depends on the number N of failures. Namely, B_i is the duration of the i-th outage in the period of interest. The quantity $B_0 = 0$ covers the case of no failures over that period, where $\Omega = \{B_0\} = \{0\}$. If there are N failures, then $\Omega \subset \mathbb{R}_+^N \cup \{0\}$. The compensation is then a function $f : \mathbb{N}_0 \times \Omega \longrightarrow \mathbb{R}_+ \cup \{0\}$ mapping the set of couples (N, B), with $B \in \Omega$, into a non-negative compensation C. The case of no failures taking place in $(0, T]$ produces no compensation, so that $f(0, 0) = 0$.

3.2   Common Compensation Policies

Number of Failures. In the simplest compensation policy the service provider pays a fixed penalty α_f for each failure occurred during the period $(0, T]$. The overall compensation during that period is then

$$C = N\alpha_f. \tag{2}$$

Number of Long Outages. That simple scheme doesn't consider that the
cost of failures is related also to how long the customer is unable to use the
service. However, very short service disruptions may be probably tolerated by the
customer, since they produce a negligible harm to it. As a first approximation,
we can assume that a failure is significant just if the outage lasts more than a
prescribed threshold ξ. In this case the compensation policy may prescribe that
no compensation is given for failures lasting less than ξ, and a fixed penalty α_{lf}
is paid for each of the other failures. The total compensation over the period
$(0, T]$ is then

$$C = \alpha_{\mathrm{lf}} \sum_{i=0}^{N} \mathbb{I}_{[B_i > \xi]}, \tag{3}$$

where $\mathbb{I}_{[x]}$ equals 1 if the condition x is satisfied and 0 otherwise. Since we have
posed $B_0 = 0$, the definition of the compensation policy (3) is valid also for
the case where there are no failures $(N = 0)$. In the following, we refer to this
compensation policy as determined by long outages.

Cumulative Duration of Outages. The compensation policy defined by (3)
takes into account the duration of outages, but is still determined by the number
of failures. It may however be the case that the damage to customers is not
negligible even for short outages, and that the overall damage is determined by
the cumulative duration of outages, regardless of whether they take place as a
large number of short outages or as a small number of long outages. Actually,
the business losses suffered due to application failures are proportional to the
duration of outages (see, e.g., Table 8.1 in [5]). In this case, we can formulate a
third compensation policy, where the total compensation is proportional to the
cumulative duration of outages over the period $(0, T]$, with a penalty α_{d} per unit
time:

$$C = \alpha_{\mathrm{d}} \sum_{i=0}^{N} B_i. \tag{4}$$

Again, when there are no failures, the above equation reduces to $C = \alpha_{\mathrm{d}} B_0 = 0$.
This compensation policy is tantamount to punish deviations from availability
target values.

4   Distribution of Losses for the Service Provider

In Section 3, we have defined three compensation policies, which relate the monetary penalty to the service quality parameters. In order to evaluate the risk
incurred by the service provider, we need to determine the probability of losses
due to the penalties paid by the service provider. In this section we provide the
probability distribution for the ON-OFF service model described in Section 2.
  We consider first the compensation policy linked to the number of failures,
which leads to the overall compensation (2). Since the unit penalty α_{f} is fixed, the
variability in the overall compensation is determined by the number of failures
occurring over the interval $[0, T]$. Since we are considering services with high

availability, the sojourn times $\{B_i\}$ in the OFF state are much shorter than those in the ON state, For the purpose of computing the number of transitions we can therefore consider as negligible the sojourn times in the OFF state, so that the number of failures can be approximated by a Poisson distribution. Over the period $[0, T]$, we have

$$\mathbb{P}[C = \alpha_f i] = \mathbb{P}[N = i] = \frac{(\lambda T)^i}{i!}e^{-\lambda T}, \qquad i = 0, 1, \dots \tag{5}$$

By applying the same Poisson approximation for the number of failures, we can compute the distribution of losses for the compensation policy based on long outages. We recall the definition (3) of the overall compensation in this case. Again, the compensation can take values in the set of multiples of the unit penalty $\{0, \alpha_{lf}, 2\alpha_{lf}, \dots\}$. Under the assumption that the durations of failures are independent of one another and of the number of failures, we obtain the probability mass function

$$
\begin{aligned}
\mathbb{P}[C = \alpha_{lf}k] &= \mathbb{P}\left[\sum_{i=0}^{N} \mathbb{I}_{[B_i > \xi]} = k\right] \qquad k \geq 1 \\
&= \sum_{j=k}^{\infty} \mathbb{P}[N = j]\mathbb{P}\left[\sum_{i=0}^{N} \mathbb{I}_{[B_i > \xi]} = k \mid N = j\right] \\
&= \sum_{j=k}^{\infty} \mathbb{P}[N = j]\mathbb{P}\left[\sum_{i=0}^{j} \mathbb{I}_{[B_i > \xi]} = k\right] \\
&= \sum_{j=k}^{\infty} \frac{(\lambda T)^j}{j!}e^{-\lambda T}\binom{j}{k}e^{-k\mu\xi}(1 - e^{-\mu\xi})^{j-k}.
\end{aligned}
\tag{6}
$$

The probability that the service provider suffers no loss is instead

$$
\begin{aligned}
\mathbb{P}[C = 0] &= \sum_{j=0}^{\infty} \frac{(\lambda T)^j}{j!}e^{-\lambda T}(1 - e^{-\mu\xi})^j \\
&= e^{-\lambda T}\sum_{j=0}^{\infty} \frac{[\lambda T(1 - e^{-\mu\xi})]^j}{j!} \\
&= e^{-\lambda T e^{-\mu\xi}}.
\end{aligned}
\tag{7}
$$

Finally, we consider the case of compensation linked to the overall duration of outages. In that case, it takes values in $\mathbb{R}_+ \cup \{0\}$. We recall the definition (4). We consider separately the cases of $N = 0$ and $N > 0$. When there are no failures, there is no compensation, and the probability of no loss is

$$\mathbb{P}[C = 0] = \mathbb{P}[N = 0] = e^{-\lambda T}. \tag{8}$$

Instead, when there are failures, the probability distribution of the compensation depends on the distribution of the sum of the individual outage durations. Since those durations are i.i.d. random variables following an exponential distribution, their sum follows an Erlang distribution; alternatively, it can be computed as the convolution of the individual exponential densities (see chapter 17.7 in [6]). When there are N failures, the probability distribution of the cumulative outage duration is then

$$\mathbb{P}\left[\sum_{i=1}^{N} B_i \leq x\right] = \int_0^x \frac{\mu^N e^{-\mu v} v^{N-1}}{(N-1)!} dv \qquad x > 0 \tag{9}$$
$$= \frac{1}{(N-1)!} \gamma(N, \mu x),$$

where $\gamma(N, x) = \int_0^x e^{-v} v^{N-1} dv$ is the lower incomplete Gamma function [7]. We have however to consider that the number of failures is random. By employing the law of total probability, and adopting the Poisson approximation for the number of failures in the period $[0, T]$, we have

$$\mathbb{P}[C \leq \alpha_{\mathrm{d}} x] = e^{-\lambda T} \sum_{i=1}^{\infty} \frac{(\lambda T)^i}{i!(i-1)!} \gamma(i, \mu x) \qquad x > 0. \tag{10}$$

5   The Value-at-Risk

The purpose of our paper is to measure the risk incurred by the service provider because of the obligations included in the SLA. Though a variety of risk measures can be adopted, we have chosen the Value-at-Risk, as it is quite widespread. In this section, we define first the Value-at-Risk, explain the motivations behind our choice, and then provide numerical results under the three compensation policies defined in Section 3.

5.1   Definition

We measure risk by the losses suffered by the service provider when it has to compensate its customers for the service disruptions according to one of the policies defined in Section 3.

A basic measure of risk could then be the maximum loss suffered over the period of interest. But that loss may be unbounded: just in two of the three compensation policies we have considered such maximum loss can be computed. In fact, the maximum loss $L_{\max}$ under the policy based on the cumulative duration of outages is simply $L_{\max} = \alpha_{\mathrm{d}} T$. We can compute the maximum loss also for the compensation policy based on the number of long outages. In fact, the maximum number of outages lasting more than ξ is $\lfloor T/\xi \rfloor$, so that the maximum loss over the period $[0, T]$ under this compensation policy is $L_{\max} = \alpha_{\mathrm{lf}} \lfloor T/\xi \rfloor$. Instead, in the case of a compensation based on the number of failures, we have, at least theoretically, unbounded losses, since we can have an infinite number of outages of infinitesimal durations.

Moreover, using the maximum loss as a measure of risk neglects any probability information. We choose therefore a risk measure that takes into account the probability distribution of losses. We borrow from the field of finance the Value-at-Risk (VaR), which represents the maximum loss that is not exceeded with a given probability [8]. Namely, for a given confidence level η, the VaR is

$$\text{VaR}_\eta = \inf\{l \in \mathbb{R} : \mathbb{P}[L > l] \leq 1 - \eta\}. \tag{11}$$

The VaR represents a natural proxy for the maximum loss when the loss is unbounded and we consider a large value for the confidence level. Actually, it is equal to the η-quantile of the distribution of losses, computed through the generalized inverse of that distribution. We need to employ the generalized inverse, since the loss may be discrete rather than continuous (hence the probability distribution is a many-to-one function).

5.2 Computation

In the case of the compensation policy based on the number of failures occurring over the period $[0, T]$, the penalty takes values on the set $\{0, \alpha_f, 2\alpha_f, \ldots\}$. Since the number of failures follows a Poisson distribution, the VaR can be obtained by computing the generalized inverse of the Poisson distribution given by Equation (5). We can plot the VaR as a function of the confidence level, obtaining a staircase curve. In Fig. 2 we report the VaR as a multiple of the unit penalty α_f, when MTTR = 4 hours, the availability is 99%, and the time horizon is one month. The value chosen for the MTTR is typical of hardware failures [9].

When we consider the policy based on the number of long outages, the distribution to invert is Equation (6). We report a sample distribution of losses in Fig. 3 when the threshold is $\xi = 0.1$ hours = 6 minutes, again for the case

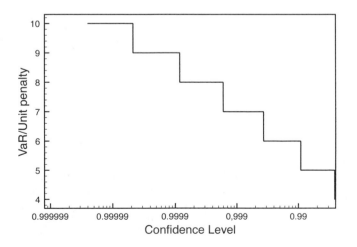

Fig. 2. Sample Value-at-Risk for the compensation policy based on the number of failures

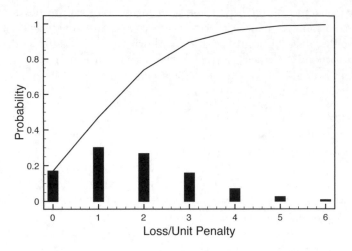

Fig. 3. Distribution of losses for the compensation policy based on the number of long outages

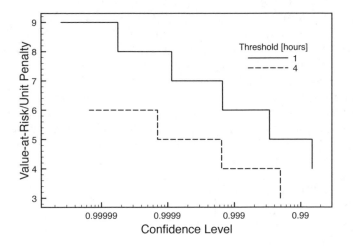

Fig. 4. Value-at-Risk for the compensation policy based on the number of long outages

where the availability is 99% and the time horizon is $T = 1$ month. We can see the impact of the threshold by plotting the VaR as the threshold is raised from 1 hour to 4 hours (the mean outage duration) in Fig. 4.

Finally, we consider the VaR when the compensation is proportional to the cumulative duration of outages. The distribution of losses is to be computed according to Equation (10). We report in Fig. 5 the distribution of losses when MTTR = 4 hours for two values of availability over $T = 1$ month. In Fig. 6 we report instead the VaR for the case of 99% availability.

As previously hinted, we can employ the VaR to compare compensation policies. In all the cases considered so far, we have plotted the normalized VaR,

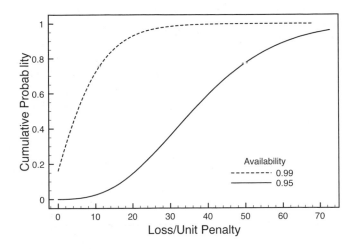

Fig. 5. Distribution of losses for the compensation policy based on the cumulative duration of outages

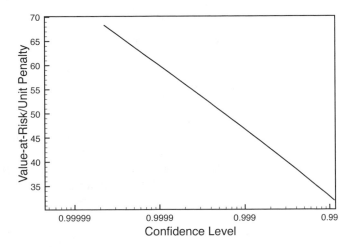

Fig. 6. Value-at-Risk for the compensation policy based on the cumulative duration of outages

expressed as a multiple of the unit penalty. The values obtained are largely different for the three compensation policies, but we also expect the unit penalties to be different as well. We must therefore find a way to compare the VaR of the three policies on an even level. For that purpose, we may set the unit penalties so to have equal mean losses under the compensation policies of interest, and compare the resulting VaR. Here, we limit ourselves to such equalization for the two compensation policies based on the number of failures and on the cumulative duration of outages, since they are more easily comparable. We can observe

that each failure lasts MTTR hours on the average, and therefore contributes to
the cumulative duration of outages by that quantity. Setting the unit penalty for
failures as $\alpha_f = \text{MTTR}\alpha_d$ would then lead to equal average losses in those two
compensation policies. We can consider the VaR obtained under that condition
as an equalized value, which can be used to directly compare the two policies.
For the value MTTR = 4 hours, employed in all the cases examined in Section
5, and for $\alpha_d = 1$ (without loss of generality for this latter condition), we obtain
the equalized VaR reported in Table 1.

Table 1. Comparison of equalized VaRs

Confidence Level [%]	VaR No. of failures	VaR Cum. duration
99	24	32.89
99.9	28	46.79
99.99	36	59.96

We can see that the the compensation policy based on the cumulative duration
exhibits a much larger equalized VaR. Hence, it is riskier: the average loss is not
enough to assess the actual risk of compensation policies.

6   Conclusions

The obligations included in Service Level Agreements may lead to significant
losses for the service provider because of the compensation policy incorporated
in the SLA. For a simple ON–OFF Markovian model for the service availability,
we have obtained analytical expressions for three different compensation policies,
based respectively on the number of failures, the number of long outages, and the
cumulative duration of outages. We have employed those expressions to derive
the Value-at-Risk, a measure of risk that gives the maximum loss that is not
exceeded with a given probability. For the cases examined, the equalized VaR
(i.e., that obtained when the mean loss is the same for the three policies) incurred
by the service provider varies heavily with the compensation policy adopted.

References

1. Cholda, P., Tapolcai, J., Cinkler, T., Wajda, K., Jajszczyk, A.: Quality of resilience as a network reliability characterization tool. IEEE Network 23(2), 11–19 (2009)
2. Moroni, S., Figueroa, N., Jofre, A., Sahai, A., Chen, Y., Iyer, S.: A Game-theoretic Framework for Creating Optimal SLA/Contract. Technical Report HPL-2007-126, HP, July 26 (2007)
3. ITU-T. Recommendation Y.1540, Internet protocol data communication service IP packet transfer and availability performance parameters (2007)

4. Martin, J., Nilsson, A.: On service level agreements for IP networks. In: Proceedings of IEEE INFOCOM 2002. Twenty-First Annual Joint Conference of the IEEE Computer and Communications Societies, vol. 2, pp. 855–863 (2002)
5. Sherif, M.H.: Managing projects in telecommunication services. John Wiley, Chichester (2006)
6. Hillier, F.S., Lieberman, G.J.: Introduction to Operations Research, 7th edn. McGraw-Hill, New York (2002)
7. Olver, F.W.J., Lozier, D.W., Boisvert, R.F., Clark, C.W. (eds.): NIST Handbook of Mathematical Functions. Cambridge University Press, Cambridge (2010)
8. McNeil, A.J., Frey, R., Embrechts, P.: Quantitative risk management: concepts, techniques and tools. Princeton University Press, Princeton (2005)
9. Chan, C.K., Chandrashekhar, U., Richman, S.H., Vasireddy, S.R.: The role of SLAs in reducing vulnerabilities and recovering from disasters. Bell Labs Technical Journal 9(2), 189–203 (2004)

Impacts of Universal Service Regulation for Broadband Internet Services*

Jeonghoon Mo[1], Weonseek Kim[2], and Dongmyung Lee[3]

[1] Dept. of Information and Industrial Engineering, Yonsei University, Seoul, Korea
j.mo@yonsei.ac.kr
[2] Dept. of Economics, Chung-Ang University, Gyeonggi-do, Korea
wnsk65@cau.ac.kr
[3] Dept. of Industrial Engineering, Seoul National University, Seoul, Korea
leoleo333@snu.ac.kr

Abstract. As more services are provided through Internet, the accessibility to Internet is becoming an essential part of modern life. In this paper, we study the impact of universal service regulation for the Internet service using an analytical model between an Internet service provider and users. We compare the regulated and unregulated situation with respect to revenue and social welfare to understand the impact of regulation. We consider both unsatruated network and saturated network cases. We find that when network is not saturated, the universal service regulation is very beneficial to the society while the benefit is not as substantial under congestion scenario.

Keywords: Pricing of the Internet Service, Flat Pricing, Usage based Pricing, Regulation.

1 Introduction

As the Internet becomes an increasingly essential part of life, access to Internet services also becomes more important. It has been widely studied that the information and communication technology (ICT) contributed to economic growth, democracy, education and cultural development [1,2,3,4]. With more application services, for instance applications for the development of electronic commerce being offered over the Internet, those who cannot access the Internet lose many opportunities, resulting in the so-called Digital Divide.

Global digital divide, the ICT difference between developed and developing countries becomes a global issues and many efforts are being made. Those poor people in developing countries do not have an access to Internet at all, which prevent them from accessing opportunities from ICT. For example, to provide the economic possibility of ICT access to the poorest 20% of the society would require reducing Internet price from $244 down to $35 per year in Mexico [7].

* This research was supported in part by the MKE under the ITRC program (NIPA-2011-(C1090-1111-0005)) and in part by NRF (2011-0002663).

J. Cohen, P. Maillé, and B. Stiller (Eds.): ICQT 2011, LNCS 6995, pp. 14–25, 2011.

To overcome the issue, projects like One Laptop per Child and 50x15 tried to provide low cost laptop computer for children in developing countries [5,6]. The United Nations is aiming to raise the awareness of the divide and formed the United Nations Global Alliance for ICT and Development and the Digital Alliance Foundation [8,9].

One way of bridging Digital Divide is through price regulation, which has been used extensively in telecommunication services. Without regulation, service providers would try to maximize the profit and they resort to pricing based discrimiation technique such as two-part tariffs or nonlinear pricing, if possible. Mackie-Mason and Varian studied pricing strategy for congestible resource such as network bandwidth and they proposed the smart market [10]. A regulator can control the situation to achieve higher social welfare and improve subscription rates by putting a ceiling on service prices. However, these achievements come at the cost of either lowered incentives for a firm to invest in its network facilities, or more congested networks [11].

Another type of price regulation is providing a baseline level of services to every resident of a country. In telephone service, it was implemented under the name of *universal service*. The telecommunication act of 1996 includes the concept of the universal services in the US and many countries provide similar type of service. Though the universal service is popular for telecommunication service, a similar service for the broadband Internet has not been implemented. Recently, US congresswoman introduced the broadband affordability act to allow low-income citizens to get more affordable broadband Internet service [12], which is being discussed.

In this paper, we study the regulation of Internet pricing by introducing a so-called basic service that a regulator can utilize to increase subscribership. Rather than simply imposing a price cap, a regulator enforces a cheaper service for a small amount of traffic volume, while leaving regular services to the firms discretion. We develop a mathematical model to show the impact of such a service. We establish that introduction of the basic service can increase subscribership without discouraging service providers significantly.

The paper is organized as follows. In section 2, we describe the framework under which we analyze the revenue, social welfare, and net-utilities. We consider both saturated and unsaturated network cases (sections 3 and 4). In section 5, we study the impact of basic service on the subscribership, which can be used by a regulator. Finally, we concluded the paper in section 6.

2   Model

We consider a system consisting of a network with capacity C and $N \gg 1$ users of the network. The users have different expectations on the network services and the perceived utility of a user that generates a traffic of volume x is

$$u(v; x) = v\sqrt{x}, \tag{1}$$

where v is a user type parameter of which distribution is uniform in $[0, 1]$. We assume $\sqrt{\cdot}$ utility function to model a decreasing marginal utility value. If the value of v is high, the user is willing to use more bandwidth since its perceived utility value is high. On the other hand, if v is low, the user is less likely to use bandwidth. If we let $x(v)$ be the traffic volume generated by user of type v, the total traffic volume T is

$$T = \int_0^1 x(v)N dv.$$

As the total traffic volume T is approaching the network capacity, user will experience system delays, which causes disutility. The perceived utility including the disutility is

$$v\sqrt{x} - d_c(T).$$

The value of $d_c(T) = 0$ for non-congested network and $d_c(T) > 0$ for congested one.

The service provider charges $p(x)$ for transmitting traffic volume x. We consider a linear pricing function $p(x) = p + \beta x$ which covers flat charge, volume-based charge and two-part tariff. If $\beta = 0$, $p(x)$ is flat; if $p = 0$, $p(x)$ is volume-based charge; Otherwise, it is a two-part tariff.

A user of type v tries to maximize its net-utility expressed by

$$v\sqrt{x} - p(x) - d_c(T),$$

which is the difference between the perceived utility and the payment. Hence, the traffic volume $x(v)$ of type v user can be obtained from the solution of

($\mathbf{P_{user}}$)

$$x(v) = arg \max_{0 \le x \le \bar{x}} [v\sqrt{x} - p(x) - d_c(T)]. \tag{2}$$

The traffic volume of all users is less than $\bar{x}$ due to limitations on the user access rate.

The service provider tries to maximize its revenue R given by $R = \int_0^1 p(x(v))dv$. Hence, the problem ($\mathbf{P_{NSP}}$) of the network service provider is

($\mathbf{P_{NSP}}$)

$$\text{maximize} \int_0^1 p(x(v))dv. \tag{3}$$

The social welfare W of the system is given by

$$W = \int_0^1 v\sqrt{x(v)}N dv - N d_c(T).$$

The provider takes R out of W and the fraction of welfare distributed to users is $W - R$. The regulator wants to guarantee the service offered by the service provider benefits both users and provider. The objective of the regulator is to balance both provider and users by balancing $\frac{R}{W}$ and $\frac{W-R}{W}$.

3   Unsaturated Network

We first consider an unsaturated network in which the number of users is relatively smaller than the network capacity. When a new service is introduced, the number of subscriptions is small and the network bandwidth is underutilized. The broadband service of many countries corresponds to this case.

In unsaturated networks, we can assume that the delay disutility function $d_c(T) = 0$ as the capacity of network C is greater than the total traffic volume T. With this assumption, we consider two different tariffs: flat and volume-based tariff.

3.1 Flat Price

Under the flat price, as the marginal cost is zero, users either generate their maximum volume $\bar{x}$ if its utility is greater than the flat price p or zero, otherwise. In other words, the rate $x(v)$ of a type v user is given by:

$$x(v) = \begin{cases} \bar{x} & \text{if } v \geq \frac{p}{\sqrt{\bar{x}}}; \\ 0 & \text{otherwise} \end{cases}$$

As the net-utility $v\sqrt{\bar{x}} - p$ is increasing in v, users with $v \geq v_0$ will subscribe to the service where $v_0 := \frac{p}{\sqrt{\bar{x}}}$. Thus the subscription ratio under the flat price is $(1 - v_0)$ or $(1 - \frac{p}{\sqrt{\bar{x}}})$. The revenue $R(p)$ of the flat price is

$$R(p) = Np\left(1 - \frac{p}{\sqrt{\bar{x}}}\right).$$

For a given flat price p, the sum of perceived utility or social welfare W is:

$$W(p) = \int_{v_0}^1 v\sqrt{\bar{x}}N dv = \frac{\sqrt{\bar{x}}}{2}\left(1 - \frac{p^2}{\bar{x}}\right)N.$$

As shown in Figure 1 (left), the revenue $R(p)$ is maximized when $p = p^*$ where $p^* = \frac{\sqrt{\bar{x}}}{2}$. At the revenue maximizing price p^*, the revenue and social welfare are given by:

$$R(p^*) = \frac{1}{4}N\sqrt{\bar{x}} \quad \text{and} \quad W(p^*) = \frac{3}{8}N\sqrt{\bar{x}}$$

respectively. The sum of net-utility or the difference $W(p^*) - R(p^*)$ is $\frac{1}{8}N\sqrt{\bar{x}}$.

Note that as the flat price p increases from 0 to p^*, the social welfare $W(p)$ decreases from $\frac{1}{2}N\sqrt{\bar{x}}$ to $\frac{3}{8}N\sqrt{\bar{x}}$, which is 25% loss of social welfare. At the same time, revenue $R(p)$ increases from 0 to $\frac{1}{4}N\sqrt{\bar{x}}$.

The ratio $\frac{R(p)}{W(p)}$ is the fraction given to the service provider out of the social welfare and after algebraic manipulation, we have

$$\frac{R}{W} = \frac{2p}{\sqrt{\bar{x}} + p}.$$

The higher the price p, the higher the ratio.

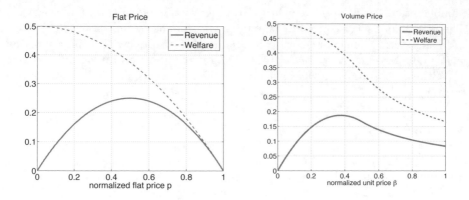

Fig. 1. The revenue and social welfare of the flat and volume price (unsaturated network)

3.2   Volume-Based Price

In this subsection, we consider a pure volume-based pricing in which the provider charges β per unit traffic i.e. $p(x) = \beta x$ without any fixed component. For a given unit charge of β, a user of type v generates $x(v)$ of traffic to maximize its net-utility $v\sqrt{x} - \beta x$, which is given by:

$$x(v) = \min\left(\frac{v^2}{4\beta^2}, \bar{x}\right).$$

The rate $x(v)$ increases quadratically with v until it reaches $\bar{x}$. The corresponding net-utility of a type v user is

$$u(x(v), v) = v\sqrt{x(v)} - \beta x(v) = \min\left(\frac{v^2}{4\beta^2}, v\sqrt{\bar{x}} - \beta\bar{x}\right).$$

The total traffic volume T generated by all users is

$$T = \int_0^1 x(v)N dv = \int_0^{v_1} \frac{v^2}{4\beta^2} N dv + \int_{v_1}^1 \bar{x}N dv \tag{4}$$

where v_1 is such that $\frac{v_1^2}{4\beta^2} = \bar{x}$ or $v_1 = 2\beta\sqrt{\bar{x}}$. After integration and rewriting, we have

$$T = \begin{cases} \left(1 - \frac{4}{3}\beta\sqrt{\bar{x}}\right)N\bar{x} & \text{if } v_1 \le 1; \\ \frac{1}{12\beta^2}N, & \text{otherwise.} \end{cases}$$

With the unit charge of β, the revenue $R(\beta)$ of provider is simply $\beta \cdot T$ or

$$R(\beta) = \begin{cases} \beta\left(1 - \frac{4}{3}\beta\sqrt{\bar{x}}\right)N\bar{x}, & \text{if } v_1 \le 1 \\ \frac{1}{12\beta}N, & \text{otherwise} \end{cases}$$

The social welfare $W(\beta)$ that can be achieved by the unit price β is

$$W(\beta) = \int_0^1 v\sqrt{x(v)}\,dv = \int_0^{v_1} \frac{v^2}{2\beta}N\,dv + \int_{v_1}^1 v\sqrt{\bar{x}}N\,dv \tag{5}$$

$$= \begin{cases} \frac{1}{2}\left(1 - \frac{4}{3}\beta^2\bar{x}\right)N\sqrt{\bar{x}} & \text{if } v_1 \leq 1; \\ \frac{1}{6\beta}N & \text{otherwise.} \end{cases} \tag{6}$$

Figure 1 (right) shows the revenue $R(\beta)$ and the social welfare $W(\beta)$ as a function of β. The x-axis corresponds to $\beta\sqrt{\bar{x}}$ between 0 and 1 and the y-axis corresponds to $\frac{R(\beta)}{\bar{x}N}$ and $\frac{W(\beta)}{N}$. As shown in Figure 1 (right), there exist unique β^* that maximizes $R(\beta)$, which is $\beta^* = \frac{3}{8\sqrt{\bar{x}}}$, with resultant revenue $R(\beta^*)$ and $W(\beta^*)$ of

$$R(\beta^*) = \frac{3}{16}N\sqrt{\bar{x}} \quad \text{and} \quad W(\beta^*) = \frac{13}{32}N\sqrt{\bar{x}}.$$

4   Saturated Network

As network services gain popularity, the number of users in the system is large enough to consume all the capacity C. In other words, $N\bar{x} > C$. The constraint $T \leq C$ becomes bottleneck in this case. Moreover, the delay $d_c(T)$ comes into play as the network capacity becomes saturated.

4.1   Flat Price

For a given flat price p, a user of type v selects her data rate $x(v)$ to maximizes her net-utility

$$v\sqrt{x} - p - d_c(T).$$

The traffic volume $x(v)$ is chosen such that $\frac{v}{2\sqrt{x}} = \delta$, so that $x = x(v) := \frac{v^2}{4\delta^2}$, where δ is a derivative of a delay disutility function $d_c(T)$. The value of δ is chosen such that the total traffic $T \leq C$ or

$$T := \int_{v_0}^1 x(v)N\,dv = \frac{1 - v_0^3}{12\delta^2}N \leq C.$$

In this analysis, we introduce the delay derivative δ to constrain traffic, but the disutility due to delay becomes negligible as soon as the traffic is slightly less than capacity. Thus, a user of type v joins the network if $v \geq v_0$, where $\frac{v_0^2}{2\delta} = p$. and $\frac{1-v_0^3}{12\delta^2} = c := \frac{C}{N}$ since the total traffic $T = C$ due to flat pricing. The revenue $R(p) = Np(1 - v_0)$ and the social welfare can be written as a function of v_0 by substituting the expressions for p and δ in R, as follows:

$$R(p(v_0)) = N\frac{v_0^2(1 - v_0)}{\sqrt{1 - v_0^3}}\sqrt{3c} \quad \text{and} \quad W(p) = \int_{v_0}^1 v\sqrt{x(v)}N\,dv = \frac{1 - v_0^3}{6\delta}N.$$

The revenue R is maximized when $v_0 \approx 0.761$. It follows that $p \approx 1.34\sqrt{c}$, $R \approx 0.32\sqrt{c}N$ and $W \approx 0.43\sqrt{c}N$ which can be seen in the left plot of Fig.2. Under this scheme, only 24% of users join the service.

4.2 Volume-Based Price

To maximize the net-utility $v\sqrt{x} - \beta x$, a user of type v generates $x(v)$ given by $x(v) = \frac{v^2}{4\beta^2}$. Note that the resulting net-utility $\frac{v^2}{4\beta}$ is always positve. Hence all users are in the system under the volume-based pricing. The total amount of traffic is then

$$T = \begin{cases} N\frac{1}{12\beta^2} & \text{if } \beta \geq \beta_0 := \frac{1}{\sqrt{12c}}; \\ C & \text{otherwise.} \end{cases}$$

since the total traffic volume $T \leq C$. The revenue $R(\beta)$ and the social welfare $W(\beta)$ is then

$$R(\beta) = \min\left(N\frac{1}{12\beta}, \beta N c\right), \quad W(\beta) = \int_0^1 x(v)N dv = \min(N\frac{1}{6\beta_0}, N\frac{1}{6\beta})$$

where the second term βNc of $R(\beta)$ is from the fact that $T \leq C$, and $\beta_0 = \frac{1}{\sqrt{12c}}$.

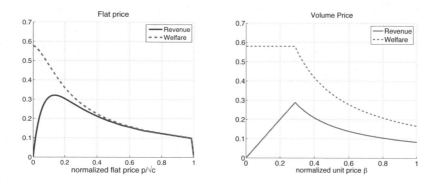

Fig. 2. The revenue and social welfare of flat and volume-based price (saturated network)

The revenue is maximized when $\beta = \beta_0$ and the revenue and social welfare at β_0 are $R(\beta_0) = 0.29N\sqrt{c}$ and $W(\beta_0) = 0.58N\sqrt{c}$, respectively.

5 Maximization of Subscribership

Traditionally, in the PSTN network, the objective of the regulator was maximizing subscribership under the name of the *universal service*. The regulator subsidizes consumers to provide the baseline level of service for all users.

Without regulation, we observed that only users of higher values of v join the service under the flat rate model as the provider sets the price level to maximize his revenue. Figure 3 shows the subscription rate for different values of price p under the flat price models. The left part of figure corresponds to the unsaturated network while the right one to the saturated one. In the unsaturated network, the subscription rate decreases linearly with price level $p\sqrt{\bar{x}}$. As the provider price is set at $\frac{1}{2}\sqrt{\bar{x}}$, the subscription rate is 50%. In the saturated network, users are more sensitive to the price level than in the unsaturated one. As they cannot transmit as much as they can, their willingness to pay is much lower than in the other case, which results in rapid decrease in subscribership. The revenue was determined at $1.34\sqrt{c}$, and the resultant subscription rate is only 24%.

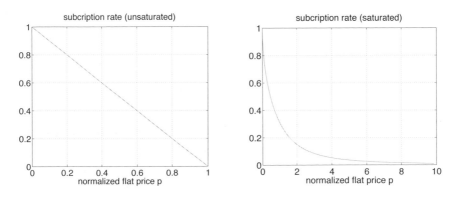

Fig. 3. Subscription Rate vs. flat price p (unsaturated network (left) and saturated network (right))

5.1   Basic Service: Unsaturated Network

To maximize the subscription rate of users, assume that the regulator forces the operator to provide a special low rate plan called *basic service* that charges a small flat price $p_1 (\ll p_2)$ for generating up to $a^2\bar{x}$ $(a \ll 1)^1$. Users who would like to generate more than $a^2\bar{x}$ use a regular service that charges p_2. Like before, we assume that $\bar{x}$ is the maximum amount of traffic that can be generated. Let v_1 and v_2 be the type parameter of a user whose net-utility value is zero for using low rate plan and regular plan, respectively. Then, $v_1 = \frac{p_1}{a\sqrt{\bar{x}}}$ and $v_2 = \frac{p_2}{\sqrt{\bar{x}}}$. As the basic service is introduced to increase the subscribership, we have $v_1 \leq v_2$ or $p_1 \leq ap_2$.

Users with $v \in [v_1, v_2)$ are eligible for the basic service only and those with $v \geq v_2$ can join either the basic or the regular service, whichever maximizes their net-utility. As the net-utility of the basic and the regular services are $u_1 = va\sqrt{\bar{x}} - p_1$ and $u_2 = v\sqrt{\bar{x}} - p_2$, u_1 is bigger if $v \leq v_3$, where $v3 = \frac{p_2-p_1}{(1-a)\sqrt{\bar{x}}}$.

Hence, users with parameter $v \in [v_1, v_3]$ will join the service the basic service and users join the regular service if $v \geq v_3$. After some calculation, we can determine the revenue and social welfare function as a function of p_1 as follows (since price p_2^* that maximizes R can be denoted as a function of p_1).

$$R(p_1, p_2^*) = N\left[\frac{(1-a)\sqrt{\bar{x}}}{4} + p_1\left(1 - \frac{p_1}{a\sqrt{\bar{x}}}\right)\right], \quad W(p_1, p_2^*) = \frac{N\sqrt{\bar{x}}}{2}\left[\frac{3+a}{4} - \frac{p_1^2}{a\bar{x}}\right].$$

---

[1] We used a^2 instead of a for computational convenience.

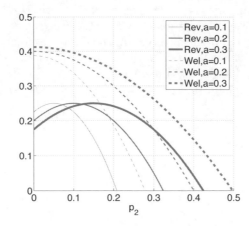

Fig. 4. Revenue and social welfare as a function of p_2 for $a = 0.1, 0.2$, and 0.3

Figure 4 shows the revenue $R(p_1, p_2^*)$ and the social welfare $W(p_1, p_2^*)$ as a function of p_2 for various values of $a = 0.1, 0.2$, and 0.3. Observe that the social welfare is higher than that of flat service $0.375N\sqrt{\bar{x}}$ but the revenue is lower than $0.25N\sqrt{\bar{x}}$. For example, consider the case in which $p_1 = 0$ or the basic service is free of charge. All users have nonnegative net-utility values and thus the subscription ratio is 100%. The revenue and social welfare reduce to $R(p_1 = 0, p_2^*) = \frac{(1-a)}{4}N\sqrt{\bar{x}}$ and $W(p_1 = 0, p_2^*) = \left(\frac{3+a}{8}\right)N\sqrt{\bar{x}}$. The revenue of the provider is smaller by $\frac{a}{4}N\sqrt{\bar{x}}$ and the social welfare is bigger by the same amount. In Figure 4, the social welfare increases with a while the revenue decreases with a when $p_1 = 0$. As the basic free service uses more bandwidth or a is bigger, the revenue of the provider decreases.

Determining (a, p_1). The maximum allowed traffic volume $a^2\bar{x}$ of the basic service should be set so the most of users can access the minimum required services. Once the value of a is determined, the flat price p_1 can be set to meet the target subscription ratio, say s. As the subscription ratio of plan 1 is $(1-v_1) = (1 - \frac{p_1}{a\sqrt{\bar{x}}})$, to meet the target subscription rate s,

$$(1 - \frac{p_1}{a\sqrt{\bar{x}}}) = s \text{ or } p_1 = (1-s)a\sqrt{\bar{x}}.$$

For example, if the target subscription rate s=100%, the price p_1 should be 0. If the target subscription rate is 90%, then $p_1 = \frac{1}{10}a\sqrt{\bar{x}}$.

In Table 1, we considered two scenarios of different target subscription ratios: 90% and 100%. We assumed that $a = 0.1$, which means that $0.01\bar{x}$ is the maximum allowed bandwidth of the basic service. To achieve 90% subscription ratio with flat service only, the price level should go down to $0.01\sqrt{\bar{x}}$, which results in very low revenue of $0.09N\sqrt{\bar{x}}$. With the basic flat service, we could achieve a 90% subscription rate with $p_1 = 0.01\sqrt{\bar{x}}$ with much higher revenue of $0.234N\sqrt{\bar{x}}$, which is very similar to the optimal revenue $0.25N\sqrt{\bar{x}}$ of the flat

Table 1. Comparison of Flat and Flat plus Basic Services(Unsaturated Network)

	Target sub.	price	T	R	W	W-R
Flat	50%	$p^* = \frac{\sqrt{\bar{x}}}{2}$	$.50N\bar{x}$	$.25N\sqrt{\bar{x}}$	$.38N\sqrt{\bar{x}}$	$.13N\sqrt{\bar{x}}$
Flat(90)	90%	$p^* = 0.1\sqrt{\bar{x}}$	$.90N\bar{x}$	$.09N\sqrt{\bar{x}}$	$.49N\sqrt{\bar{x}}$	$.41N\sqrt{\bar{x}}$
Flat +basic(90)	90%	$p_1 = .01\sqrt{\bar{x}}, p_2 = .46\sqrt{\bar{x}}$	$.50N\bar{x}$	$.23N\sqrt{\bar{x}}$	$.39N\sqrt{\bar{x}}$	$.15N\sqrt{\bar{x}}$
Volume	100%	$\beta^* = \frac{0.375}{\sqrt{\bar{x}}}$	$.50N\bar{x}$	$.19N\sqrt{\bar{x}}$	$.41N\sqrt{\bar{x}}$	$.28N\sqrt{\bar{x}}$
Flat + basic (100)	100%	$p_1 = 0, p_2 = .45\sqrt{\bar{x}}$	$.51N\bar{x}$	$.23N\sqrt{\bar{x}}$	$.40N\sqrt{\bar{x}}$	$.18N\sqrt{\bar{x}}$

service. We can observe that very high subscription ratio can be achieved with small cost to the service provider. In the second scenario of 100% target ratio, we compared the volume-based price with the flat+basic service. This can be done by providing free basic service ($p_1 = 0$). Observe that the revenue of the flat+basic service is higher than that of the volume-based one.

5.2 Basic Service: Saturated Network

Consider the saturated network case in which only 24% is the subscription ratio when the provider maximizes its revenue with the flat price. To increase the subscribership, reduction of the flat price p can be considered. However, as can be seen from Figure 3, to achieve 90% subscription ratio with flat service only, the price level should go down to $0.017\sqrt{c}$ and the revenue loss is about 98% of the maximum revenue.

Assume that the basic service is provided with price p_1 and the regular flat service is provided at price p_2. The maximum allowed traffic volume of the basic service is a^2c. A user of type v can select between the two services, whichever maximizes her net-utility. The net-utility of the basic service is given by $va\sqrt{c} - p_1$ and that of the regular service is $v\sqrt{x(v)} - p_2 = \frac{v^2}{2\delta} - p_2$. A user of type v selects the basic service if $v_1 \leq v \leq v_3$ where $v_1 a\sqrt{c} = p_1$ and $v_3 a\sqrt{c} - p_1 = \frac{v_3^2}{2\delta} - p_2$. Users with type $v \geq v_3$ select the regular service as the regular service provides higher net-utilities.

Similarly given the basic service parameter (p_1, a^2c), R can be represented as a function of v_3 only. The v_3^* that maximizes R can be found numerically. From v_3^*, we can find δ and p_2.

Assume that the maximum allowed bandwidth of the basic service $a^2c = 0.1c$. Note that the basic service parameter a of the saturated network is higher than that of the unsaturated network as c is smaller than $\bar{x}$. In Table 2, we compare the flat service with and without the basic service. We consider the target subscription ratio of 90% and 100%. If we consider target subscription ratio of 90%, the p_1 should be $(1 - 0.9)a\sqrt{c} = 0.1\sqrt{0.1}\sqrt{c} = 0.0316\sqrt{c}$. The optimal v_3^* that maximizes revenue turned out to be 0.802, i.e. the fraction of the regular service users is 19.8% with the revenue of $0.2839N\sqrt{c}$. Note that almost 70% of users rely on the basic service in this case, which seems to be quite high number. We observe the similar numbers in the next row when the target subscription ratio is 100%. The price for the basic service is 0. The revenue and welfare are very similar.

Table 2. Comparison of Flat and Flat plus Basic Services(Saturated Network)

	Taget sub.	$1 - v_3$	price	T	R	W	W-R
Flat	24%	24%	$p^* = 1.34\sqrt{c}$	Nc	$.32N\sqrt{c}$	$.43N\sqrt{c}$	$.11N\sqrt{c}$
Flat +basic(90)	90%	19.8%	$p_1 = .04\sqrt{c}, p_2 = 1.3\sqrt{c}$	Nc	$.29N\sqrt{c}$	$.49N\sqrt{c}$	$.20N\sqrt{c}$
Volume	100%	-	$\beta^* = 0.29/\sqrt{c}$	Nc	$.29N\sqrt{c}$	$.58N\sqrt{c}$	$.29N\sqrt{c}$
Flat +basic(100)	100%	19.6%	$p_1 = 0, p_2 = 1.29\sqrt{c}$	Nc	$.25N\sqrt{c}$	$.49N\sqrt{c}$	$.23N\sqrt{c}$

In the unsaturated network, the introduction of the basic service helps increasing the number of subscriptions. However, when the network is saturated, it is not as helpful. It turns out that the volume based pricing is better off than the introduction of the basic service as shown in the Table 2

6 Conclusions

In this paper, we studied different pricing schemes: flat, and volume-based under both saturated and unsaturated network environments. We introduced an analytical model in which users and an ISP are selfish i.e., try to maximize the net-utility or the revenue. We compared the impacts of different schemes. Our findings are as follows:

- In the unsaturated network environment, the flat pricing is better-off than the volume-based one for the service provider as it generates higher revenue. However, the subscribership is only 50%, which can be improved by introduction of the basic service.
- In the saturated network environment, the revenue of the flat pricing is higher than that of the volume-based one. However, it suffers severely from the subscription ratio of 24%. The volume-based one is much better-off with respect to the social welfare, which achieves 100% subscription ratio.
- Introduction of the basic service is more beneficial in the unsaturated network than in the saturated network. In the saturated network, the volume-based pricing is better-off than the basic service with respect to the social welfare and revenue.

We believe that the proposed model can be extended in many different aspects by considering more general pricing structures, and can be used to model other regulatory behaviors, which will be our future research directions.

References

1. Cole, S.: The global impact of information technology. World Development 14, 10–11, 1277–1292 (1986)
2. Banisar, D.: Freedom of information around the world: A global survey of access to government information laws. Privacy International (2006),
   http://www.freedominfo.org/documents/global_survey2006.pdf   (retrieved August 3, 2009)

3. Marshall, S., Taylor, W.: Editorial: ICT for education and training. International Journal of Education and Development using Information and Communication Technology 2(4), 3–5 (2006)
4. Castells, M.: The power of identity: The information age. In: Economy, Society and Culture, 2nd edn. The information age, vol. II, Wiley Blackwell (2004)
5. One Laptop per Child Project, http://laptop.org/en/
6. 50x15 foundation, http://50x15.org/
7. Hilbert, M.: When is Cheap, Cheap Enough to Bridge the Digital Divide? Modeling Income Related Structural Challenges of Technology Diffusion in Latin America. World Development 38(5), 756–770 (2010)
8. Global Alliance for ICT and Development, http://www.un-gaid.org/
9. Digital Alliance Foundation: Information and Communication Technology (ICT) Education for All (EFA), http://www.ictefa.org/
10. Mackie-Mason, J.K., Varian, H.R.: Pricing Congestible Network Resources. IEEE Journal of Selected Areas in Communications 13, 1141–1149 (1995)
11. Shy, O.: The Economics of Network Industries. Cambridge University Press, Cambridge (2001)
12. Matsui, S.: H.R. 3646: Broadband Affordability Act (2009), http://www.govtrack.us/congress/bill.xpd?bill=h111-3646
13. Jamshed, M.: A Conceptual Framework for the Role of Governments in Bridging the Digital Divide. Journal of Global Information Technology Management 8, 28 (2005)
14. Wallsten, S.: Regulation and Internet Use In Developing Countries. Economic Development & Cultural Change 53, 501–524 (2005)

A Token Pricing Scheme for Internet Services*

Dongmyung Lee[1], Jeonghoon Mo[2], Jean Walrand[3], and Jinwoo Park[1]

[1] Dept. of Industrial Engineering, Seoul National University, Seoul, Korea
leoleo333,autofact@snu.ac.kr
[2] Dept. of Information and Industrial Engineering, Yonsei University, Seoul, Korea
j.mo@yonsei.ac.kr
[3] Dept. of EECS, University of California, Berkeley, CA, USA
wlr@eecs.berkeley.edu

Abstract. Flat-rate pricing has been the dominant scheme for tariffing Internet services due to its popularity and simplicity. However, this scheme does not provide incentives for users to use network resources efficiently. As the demand for wireless video and other resource-intensive services grows faster than the providers' ability to expand the network capacity, this inefficiency becomes critical. This situation has led numerous researchers and practitioners to explore new pricing schemes. In this spirit, we introduce a pricing scheme called *Token Pricing* that is both practical and efficient. As in flat-rate pricing, the users face a fixed price. However, users consume tokens when they want a higher quality of service while the network is congested. This mechanism encourages users to congest the network only when they have a high utility for the service. As a result, users make a better use of the resources and the social welfare increases.

Keywords: Internet pricing, Flat-rate pricing, Token pricing, QoS.

1 Introduction

Researchers have proposed many pricing schemes for the Internet [1,2,3]. *Flat-rate pricing* is the most widely used scheme. The users pay a fixed monthly fee and get an unmetered access. The main advantages of this model are its low administrative and billing costs for the ISP as well as predictability for the users.

An *usage-based pricing* scheme charges users based on the amount of data they use [5]. Rates may vary depending on the time of day to encourage a smoother utilization of the available bandwidth resources [4]. However, such a scheme requires ISPs to monitor accurately each user's utilization and to implement a detailed billing scheme based on these measurements. Users face a variable bill and may get discouraged to use the network.

As more and more Internet services require a different level of quality of service (QoS), numerous techniques have been proposed to provide differentiated service

---

* This research was supported in part by the MKE under the ITRC program (NIPA-2011-(C1090-1111-0005)) and in part by NRF (2011-0002663).

J. Cohen, P. Maillé, and B. Stiller (Eds.): ICQT 2011, LNCS 6995, pp. 26–37, 2011.

levels. Some of these proposals use pricing mechanisms to improve the economic efficiency [1,6]. However, many of these schemes are complicated and/or involve substantial costs in both development and operations [2].

In their recent analysis, Schwartz et. al. [7] show that the transition to multiple service classes is socially desirable but may increase the cost for some users for the same level of service. To limit this undesirable effect, they propose a regulation which sets an upper bound on the fraction of the network capacity reserved for high priority service. They show that this regulation can limit the distributional consequences while enabling providers to increase their revenue. However, this scheme uses differentiated pricing, which requires traffic monitoring and may face resistance from users and providers.

In this paper, we propose a pricing scheme called 'Token Pricing' that has the advantages of flat-rate pricing, yet promotes a more efficient usage of the network resources.

2   Token Pricing Scheme

When using *token pricing*, users pay a fixed monthly fee for Internet access. Each user receives a number of *tokens*. The provider offers a high-quality Service 1 and a normal-quality Service 2. For instance, the services could correspond to different "bearers" (GBR[1] or non-GBR) in an LTE network [11].

Service 2 requires no tokens but may become congested. On the other hand, Service 1 requires some tokens and, consequently, is likely to be less congested than Service 2, thus offering a better quality by a Paris Metro pricing effect [2]. Since the number of tokens is limited, users have an incentive to use Service 1 when they derive a sufficiently higher utility from that service. Consequently, we can expect the social welfare of the network to increase since valuable resources get used for more valued applications.

A secure agent in the user's browser can monitor the token usage so that the provider does not face much additional complexity. Also, the provider does not need additional billing mechanisms.

Below, we model the token pricing scheme and the behavior of users and we analyze the improvement in social welfare. For simplicity, the analysis proceeds in three steps. Sections 2.1 and 2.2 consider discrete time models and explores the optimal strategy for a user who maximizes his total discounted utility. Section 2.1 ignores the effect of users on the congestion of the network. Section 2.2 extends the analysis to include the congestion effect. Section 2.3 studies a continuous time model for a user who maximizes his long-term average utility. That section builds on the results of the previous two. Due to the page limit, the proofs for all the theorems are in [13].

2.1   Fixed Congestion

This section studies the behavior of a user facing token pricing. For simplicity, the model is in discrete time. Time is divided in epochs, such as ten-minute

---

[1] GBR: Guaranteed Bit Rate.

intervals for instance. During each epoch, the user accesses the Internet once for an application such as a file download, a voice or video call, an email session or web browsing. The added value for the user of using the high-quality Service 1 compared to using Service 2 depends on the application.

With the token pricing scheme, each user can use Service 1 only once every K epochs, on average. The user must choose when to use Service 1. The intuition is that the user will use Service 1 only when he benefits sufficiently from that valuable service. For instance, the user may choose Service 1 for an important video call instead of wasting his tokens for a file download that can be delayed. Consequently, for a given level of congestion of Service 1, one may expect the users to benefit more from that service than under a flat pricing scheme. The analysis confirms that intuition.

Every epoch n, each user gets 1 token and faces some application whose utility is x_n higher for Service 1 than for Service 2. The x_n's are independent and identically distributed random variables. It costs K tokens per epoch to use Service 1.

Assume that the user has s tokens. The maximal total expected discounted value $V(s)$ for the user of having s tokens satisfies the following dynamic programming equation:

$$V(s) = E[\max\{\beta V(s+1), x + \beta V(s+1-K)\}]$$

where $V(s) = -\infty$ for $s < 0$ (so that the user cannot use tokens when he has fewer than K). In this expression $\beta \in (0,1)$ is the discount factor.

The optimal policy is then to use K tokens if and only if

$$x + \beta V(s+1-K) > \beta V(s+1),$$

i.e., if and only if

$$x > a(s) := \beta[V(s+1) - V(s+1-K)].$$

Thus, as expected, the user chooses to use Service 1 only for applications that benefit sufficiently from that service. As the next result shows, the user is more likely to use Service 1 when he has accumulated many tokens, which is not surprising.

Theorem 1. $a(s)$ *is nonincreasing.*

2.2   Variable Congestion

In this section, we consider that the value of Service 1 for an application characterized by x as before is $g(x,p)$, where p is the congestion level of Service 1. The interpretation is that, as it gets more congested, Service 1 becomes less valuable compared to Service 2. Thus, $g(x,p)$ is decreasing in p and nondecreasing in x.

The maximal total expected discounted value $V(s,p)$ for a user facing a Service 1 with congestion level p when he has s tokens satisfies the following dynamic programming equations:

$$V(s,p) = E[\max\{\beta V(s+1,p), g(x,p) + \beta V(s+1-K,p)\}].$$

The congestion level p is the fraction of users who use Service 1. Thus, the value of p is a function of the behavior of the users and we will consider that p is the probability that a given user uses Service 1. The interpretation is that there are many users in the system and that each user faces the congestion that many other users generate for Service 1. By himself, one user has a negligible influence on the congestion level of Service 1. Thus, this model can be thought of as a mean-field limit of the system when the number of users increases.

To analyze this model numerically, we need an estimate of p. This requires an estimate of the distribution of s. Now, s is a Markov chain that increases by 1 with probability $1 - p$ and decreases by $K - 1$ otherwise. The state-transition diagram of this Markov chain is shown in Figure 1.

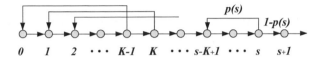

Fig. 1. The Markov chain $\{s_n, n \geq 0\}$

The transition probability matrix of this Markov chain is such that, for $s \geq K$,

$$p(s, p) = P(s, s - K + 1, p) = 1 - P(s, s + 1, p)$$
$$= P[\beta V(s + 1, p) < g(x, p) + \beta V(s + 1 - K, p)] =: P[x > a(s, p)].$$

Also, for $s \leq K - 1$,
$$P(s, s + 1, p) = 1.$$

The following result is similar to Theorem 1.

Theorem 2. $a(s, p)$ *is nonincreasing in* s.

As we discussed earlier, p is the probability that a user uses Service 1. If we knew p, we could calculate the transition probabilities. These correspond to some stationary distribution for s. One could then determine p from the following fixed point equation:

$$p = E[p(s, p)] \tag{1}$$

The following theorem shows that the fixed point exists and is unique.

Theorem 3. $E[p(s, p)]$ *has a unique fixed point* $p = \frac{1}{K}$.

2.3   Continuous Time

In this section, we consider that a user gets M tokens per day and it costs 1 token for using Service 1. Applications arrive as a Poisson process with rate λ during the day where each has a utility that is higher by x for using Service 1 instead of Service 2. We assume that x is an exponentially distributed random variable with mean 1 and is independent across applications.

The user can hold his tokens and use them whenever he wants. To maximize the long-term average value of his tokens, the user adopts a stationary Markov policy that is of a threshold type. This follows from the fact that the optimal policy for a total discounted cost is of that type and that the policy converges to the optimal long-term average cost policy as the discount factor β goes to 1, as shown in [12].

As a result, the user uses one token if $g(x, q_1) > \gamma$ where

$$P[g(x, q_1) > \gamma] = \frac{M}{\lambda} = \exp\{-\widehat{\gamma}\}$$

where $q_1 = M/c$ is the congestion level in Service 1, and $\widehat{\gamma} = g_{q_1}^{-1}(\gamma)$.

The value per token (i.e., the expected value of a single application in token scheme) is then

$$R(M, \lambda) := E[g(x, q_1) : g(x, q_1) > \gamma] = E[g(x, q_1) : X > \widehat{\gamma}].$$

Then the total value generated by the token scheme is

$$MR(M, \lambda).$$

3   Numerical Analysis

In this section, we provide some numerical results to see how the value of the token scheme changes with respect to the variables K or M that determine the cost of Service 1.

3.1   Discrete Epochs

To see how the value differs with respect to the number of tokens required to use Service 1, we set up a numerical experiment with a two specific utility functions as follows:

$$g_1(x, p) = x - \eta p, \quad g_2(x, p) = \frac{x}{\eta(p + 1)} - \epsilon.$$

In these expressions, η denotes the number of users in a given network. In other words, since p denotes the fraction of users using service 1, ηp represents the actual congestion in the network that affects the user utility. Here, $\epsilon > 0$ makes the utility negative when the congestion is severe. Without that term, the utility g_2 would always be positive, independently of the congestion level.

Figure 2(a), 2(b) shows the expected value of the token pricing scheme with 5 different congestion levels (η). We see that when the number of users in the network is low the overall value is high since the congestion disutility is low. Also there exists some $K = K^*$ that produces the highest value when the network is not under-utilized. However, when ones increases K beyond K^*, the value decreases since users get to use Service 1 for fewer applications.

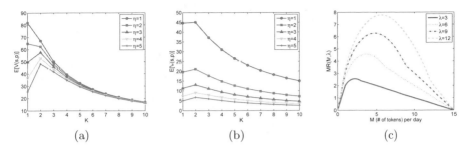

Fig. 2. Values of Token pricing scheme with respect to K or M: (a) $g_1(x,p)$, (b) $g_2(x,p)$; (c) $g_3(x,q)$

3.2   Continuous Time

For the continuous time model we consider the following utility function $g_3(x,q)$:

$$g_3(x,q) = x - q.$$

Then we have

$$R(M,\lambda) = 1 - \frac{M}{c} + \max\{0, \log \frac{\lambda}{M}\}.$$

Figure 2(c) illustrates the value $MR(M,\lambda)$ of the token scheme with respect to M for various demand values λ. We observe that there is an optimal number M of tokens that maximizes the user utility. In addition, we see that when user demand increases it is better to let users use premium service more (higher optimal M) as long as the total utility surplus produced by using multiple of files in service 1 is larger than the disutility due to congestion. Therefore, if the provider increases M larger than the optimal value given fixed demand (λ), the value tends to decrease as the disutility coming from congestion increases. Thus operators who adopt the token scheme should adjust the number of tokens.

4   Flat vs Token

In the previous section, we have analyzed the proposed token pricing scheme and illustrated its characteristics. We observed that it is simple for both the provider and the users. In addition, we have seen that the token scheme increases user welfare by letting users accumulate tokens and use them only for relatively more valuable applications.

In this section we validate our proposed scheme by comparing it with flat-rate pricing. Each day, the user uses λ applications, on average, and each is of type x, an exponentially distributed random variable with mean κ, independent across applications. In all cases, we use the same model for the increase $g(x,q)$ in utility of using Service 1 instead of Service 2 when the congestion level of Service 1 is q and the application is of type x:

$$g(x,q) = A - xq.$$

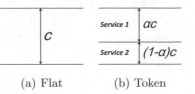

(a) Flat   (b) Token

Fig. 3. Network capacity for Flat and Token pricing scheme with two service classes

In this expression, A denotes a positive benefit for receiving Internet service, which is independent of the pricing scheme.

First, consider flat-rate pricing. Assume that the congestion level of the flat-rate network is q_f. The total average daily value created by flat-pricing is

$$W(\lambda) = \lambda E[g(x, q_f)] = \lambda(A - \kappa q_f)$$

since there are λ applications per day, on average.

For the token scheme, the operator chooses the portion α of capacity to be allocated for Service 1 (respectively, $1-\alpha$ for Service 2). The user decides whether to use Service 1 or Service 2 depending on the application type x. Assume that the congestion level of Service i is q_i, for $i = 1, 2$, with $q_1 < q_2$. Then, as we saw in Section 2.3, the user uses Service 1 if

$$g(x, q_1) - g(x, q_2) = x(q_2 - q_1) > \gamma \tag{2}$$

where the threshold γ is such that

$$P[x(q_2 - q_1) > \gamma] = \exp\{-\frac{\kappa \gamma}{q_2 - q_1}\} = \frac{M}{\lambda}.$$

Solving this equation allows to derive γ. We find $\gamma = -\frac{q_2 - q_1}{\kappa} \log\{\frac{M}{\lambda}\}$. Note that γ decreases with the fraction M/λ of applications that can use Service 1.

Since the value of the token scheme comes from two services, the total average value is given by

$$S(M, \alpha, \lambda) = \underbrace{M.E[g(x, q_1)|x(q_2 - q_1) > \gamma]}_{Service\ 1\ utility} + \underbrace{(\lambda - M)E[g(x, q_2)|x(q_2 - q_1) < \gamma]}_{Service\ 2\ utility}.$$

The provider using the token scheme chooses the number M of tokens per day and the capacity ratio α that maximizes the value to users. Thus the total value $R(\lambda)$ of using the token scheme is as follows:

$$R(\lambda) = \max_{M, \alpha} S(M, \alpha, \lambda).$$

The value of any pricing scheme would depend upon the service type the users are using. The service types could be classified into two categories [9]: capacity-sharing service and latency-based service.

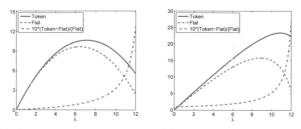

(a) Capacity Sharing Service (b) Latency Based Service

Fig. 4. Comparison of Flat and Token pricing scheme with two service classes $(A=3)$

4.1 Capacity-Sharing Service

First, we consider a generic class of services, in which the total demand in a network is distributed among the processors with some fixed total capacity (per user) c. Thus, we define the congestion functions as:

$$q_f = \frac{\lambda}{c}, \quad q_1 = \frac{M}{\alpha c}, \quad q_2 = \frac{\lambda - M}{(1-\alpha)c}$$

This type of congestion function is considered in prior work [8]. The interpretation is that if N applications share a capacity C, then each application faces a congestion disutility N/C. Accordingly, the value of the token scheme is

$$
\begin{aligned}
S_{CS}(M,\alpha,\lambda) &= ME[g(\theta,q_1)|\Pi] + (\lambda - M)E[g(\theta,q_2)|\Pi^c] \\
&= M\left[A - \frac{\lambda\kappa}{\alpha c}\left(\frac{M}{\lambda}\right)^\kappa\left(1 + \log\left(\frac{\lambda}{M}\right)^\kappa\right)\right] \\
&\quad + (\lambda - M)\left[A - \frac{\lambda\kappa}{(1-\alpha)c}\left\{1 - \left(\frac{M}{\lambda}\right)^\kappa\left(1 + \log\left(\frac{\lambda}{M}\right)^\kappa\right)\right\}\right].
\end{aligned}
$$

where Π is the event that a user uses Service 1 as in (2).

4.2 Latency-Based Services

In other services, latency may be a major concern. A simple model to capture the latency is by using an M/M/1 queue model [9]. Using this model, we define a congestion function for latency-based services as follows:

$$\text{Total expected delay} = \frac{1}{\mu - \lambda}$$

where λ is the arrival rate and μ is the service rate. This function captures the fact that when the network utilization gets close to the whole capacity, the delay goes to infinity. Then, assuming the service rate is the available capacity, the congestion functions for each of the services (Flat and Token) are

$$q_f = \frac{1}{c-\lambda}, \quad q_1 = \frac{1}{\alpha c - \lambda/M}, \quad q_2 = \frac{1}{(1-\alpha)c - \lambda(1-1/M)}.$$

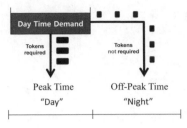

Peak Time   Off-Peak Time

"Day"   "Night"

Fig. 5. Token scheme with Single Class: A single day is divided into two time zones

This type of congestion has been considered in prior work [10] as well. Hence the value of Token scheme in this type of service is

$$S_{LB}(M, \alpha, \lambda) = ME[g(\theta, q_1)|\Pi] + (\lambda - M)E[g(\theta, q_2)|\Pi^c]$$

$$= M\left[A - q_1\frac{\lambda\kappa}{M}\left(\frac{M}{\lambda}\right)^{\kappa}\left(1 + \log\left(\frac{\lambda}{M}\right)^{\kappa}\right)\right] +$$

$$(\lambda - M)\left[A - \frac{q_2\lambda\kappa}{\lambda - M}\left\{1 - \left(\frac{M}{\lambda}\right)^{\kappa}\left(1 + \log\left(\frac{\lambda}{M}\right)^{\kappa}\right)\right\}\right]$$

Figure 6(a) and 6(b) show the numerical results for capacity sharing service and latency based service respectively. From the comparison, we see that, irrespective of service types, the token scheme always produces higher revenue than flat-rate pricing. Moreover, we observe that the surplus created by the token scheme should become more advantageous for future wireless Internet tariffing since, in the future, we expect (1) a drastic increase in wireless data traffic and (2) a much higher portion of delay-sensitive multimedia services.

5   Token Scheme with Single Class

In this section, we consider the Token scheme with single class instead of two service classes. We divide one day into two different time zones: peak time and off-peak time. We will use the notation 'Day' for peak time, and 'Night' for off-peak time since usually the network is more congested in day time. (However, this is just for the explanatory pupose and thus the peak/off-peak time could be some time segments during the day.)

Users pay a (fixed) monthly fee and are given some amount of tokens as before. For simplicity, we only consider the demand in Day time since these traffic contributes to the network overload while the network at Night is under-utilized. Unlike the previous case, using 'tokens,' here, means using the service right now (i.e., Day time) instead of at Night. Since the number of tokens is limited, users will use the tokens only when the utility gain of using that service at Day instead of at Night is sufficiently large, which will, possibly, lead to a load balancing of the network traffic between peak and off-peak hours.

Considers a case where user's decision is to use tokens and enjoy the service now (for their day time demand) and, if not, delay the service to Night time. Since he uses the service either at Day or Night, his decision to use tokens is based on the utility x, the day time congestion p_D, and the night time congestion p_N, where $p_D + p_N = 1$. Here the utility x is not an 'added' utility of using the service at Day, instead, it denotes the 'absolute' utility of the services that is supposed to use at Day time when Token scheme is not used (i.e., day time demand) and it is an independent and identically distributed random variable. As for the two-service classes case, a user gets one token per day and it requires K tokens to use the service at Day time. Thus the maximal total expected discounted value $V(s, p_D)$ for the user of having s tokens facing the congestions in both time period (i.e., p_D and p_N) satisfies the following dynamic programming equations:

$$V(s, p_D) = E[\max\{g_N(x, p_N) + \beta V(s+1, p_D), g_D(x, p_D) + \beta V(s+1-K, p_D)\}].$$

$g_D(x, p)$ denotes the perceived Day time utility function where the service type of x is used at Day time facing the congestion p. Likewise, $g_N(x, p)$ is the perceived night time utility function. To represent the higher utility for using at Day time we have

$$\frac{\partial g_D(x, p)}{\partial x} > \frac{\partial g_N(x, p)}{\partial x} \tag{3}$$

Also, as in the two-class case, the perceived utility functions $g_D(x, p_D)$ and $g_N(x, p_N)$ is decreasing in congestion p_D and p_N respectively, i.e.,

$$\frac{\partial g_D(x, p_D)}{\partial p_D} < 0, \quad \frac{\partial g_N(x, p_N)}{\partial p_N} < 0 \tag{4}$$

The optimal policy is to use K tokens if and only if,

$$g_N(x, p_N) + \beta V(s+1, p_D) < g_D(x, p_D) + \beta V(s+1-K, p_D)$$
$$\Leftrightarrow \beta\{V(s+1, p_D) - V(s+1-K, p_D)\} < g_D(x, p_D) - g_N(x, p_N)$$
$$\Leftrightarrow \beta\{V(s+1, p_D) - V(s+1-K, p_D)\} < \widehat{g}(x, p_D) \quad \Leftrightarrow \quad x > \widehat{a}(s, p_D)$$

where we define the function $\widehat{g}(x, p_D) := g_D(x, p_D) - g_N(x, p_N)$ and $\widehat{a}(s, p_D) = \widehat{g}_{p_D}^{-1}(\beta\{V(s+1, p_D) - V(s+1-K, p_D)\})$.

Now the optimal policy depends on two variables x and p_D instead of three (x, p_D, p_N), since $p_D + p_N = 1$. Also, $\widehat{g}(x, p_D)$ is increasing in x and decreasing in p_D since $\frac{\partial \widehat{g}(x, p_D)}{\partial x} = \frac{\partial g_D(x, p)}{\partial p_D} - \frac{\partial g_N(x, p)}{\partial x} > 0$ from (3) and $\frac{\partial \widehat{g}(x, p_D)}{\partial p_D} = \frac{\partial g_D(x, p)}{\partial p_D} + \frac{\partial g_N(x, p)}{\partial p_N} < 0$ from (4).

Hence, the optimal policy is mathematically equivalent to the two-class service case with variable congestion (as in Sec. 2.2) except that the notation has changed from the congestion in Service 1, p, to the congestion in Day time, p_D and from the utility function $g(x, p)$ to $\widehat{g}(x, p_D)$. Thus, Theorems 2 and 3 hold for this case as well.

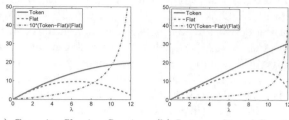

(a) Capacity Sharing Service   (b) Latency Based Service

Fig. 6. Comparison of Flat and Token pricing scheme with single service class (A=3)

5.1   Comparison with Flat and Token with Single Service Class

This section validates the Token Scheme with single service class by comparing with Flat pricing as well. Each day, the user has λ applications to use at peak time (i.e., Day time demand), on average, and each is of type x, an exponentially distributed random variable with mean κ, independent across applications. Also it requires 1 token to use the service at Day time. For this scheme, using tokens means using the service at Day so each user will use M applications, on average, at Day time and the rest $\lambda - M$ at Night. The only difference with the two service classes case is that the capacity is not divided in any way since there is merely a single service. Thus the network capacity is c for both Day and Night.

For Flat pricing, as there is no cost for using the service at Day, all the Day time demand is used at peak time. This means that all the Day time demand (λ) is used at peak time and none at night. From Fig. 6 we see that, similar to the two service classes case, Token sheme is superior to Flat scheme for both capacity sharing service and latency based service.

6   Conclusions

The design of tariff schemes for packet-based network services should not only take into account various aspects to make it technologically feasible but also consider social issues from the perspective of users to be actually used in practice. Researchers have proposed numerous pricing schemes to provide QoS since, in the future, we expect a rapid increase in the applications that require high QoS. Nevertheless, most of the schemes are too complicated and, above all, unfavored by users. In this spirit, we proposed a novel scheme called, Token pricing scheme, in a way that is simple and predictive to be well appreciated by users, and also efficient to provide QoS requirements. We have shown for both single service and two service classes that, comparing with the current dominant Flat-rate pricing, our proposed scheme gives higher utility to the users, and especially significant increase of utility surplus for Latency based services, with relatively low cost of implementation.

References

1. MacKie-Mason, J., Varian, H.: Pricing congestible network resources. IEEE Journal on Selected Areas in Communications 13(7), 1141–1149 (1995)
2. Odlyzko, A.: Paris metro pricing and for the Internet. In: AT&T Labs, Research, New Jersey, U.S.A (May 1999)
3. Joe-Wong, C., Ha, S., Chiang, M.: Time-dependent Broadband pricing. In: Information Theory and Applications Workshop (February 2011)
4. Chowdhury, R.H.: Internet pricng, TKK T-110.5190 Seminar on Internetworking (2006)
5. Altmann, J., Chunen, K.: How to charge for network services - flat-rate or usage-based? Computer Networks 36, 519–531 (2001)
6. Semret, N., Liao, R.R.-F., Campbell, A.T., Lazar, A.A.: Pricing, provisioning and peering: dynamic markets for differentiated Internet services and implications for network interconnections. IEEE Journal on Selected Areas in Communications 18, 2499–2513 (2000)
7. Schwartz, G., Shetty, N., Walrand, J.: Impact of QoS on Internet User Welfare. In: Papadimitriou, C., Zhang, S. (eds.) WINE 2008. LNCS, vol. 5385, pp. 716–723. Springer, Heidelberg (2008)
8. Gibbens, R., Mason, R., Steinberg, R.: Internet Service Classes under Competition. IEEE Journal on Selected Areas in Communications 18, 2490–2498 (2000)
9. Chau, C.-K., Wang, Q., Chiu, D.-M.: On the Viability of Paris Metro Pricing for Communication and Service Networks. In: Proc. INFOCOM (2000)
10. Ros, D., Tuffin, B.: A mathematical model of the Paris Metro pricing scheme for charging packet networks. Computer Networks 46, 73–85 (2004)
11. Ekstrom, H.: QoS Constrol in the 3GPP Evolved Packet System. IEEE Communications Magazine 47, 76–83 (2009)
12. Ross, S.: An Introduction to Stochastic Dynamic Programming. Academic Press, London (1983)
13. Lee, D., Mo, J., Walrand, J.: A Token Pricing Scheme for Internet Services, Technical Report, http://nemo.yonsei.ac.kr/~jhmo/nemo/Research_files/Token_TechRep.pdf

Exploring User-Provided Connectivity – A Simple Model*

Mohammad Hadi Afrasiabi and Roch Guérin

University of Pennsylvania, Philadelphia PA 19104, USA
afram@seas.upenn.edu, guerin@ee.upenn.edu

Abstract. The advent of cheap and ubiquitous wireless access has introduced a number of new connectivity paradigms. This paper investigates one of them, *user-provided connectivity* or UPC. In contrast to traditional infrastructure-based connectivity, *e.g.*, connectivity through the up-front build-out of expensive base-stations, UPC realizes connectivity organically as users join and expand its coverage. The low(er) deployment cost this affords is one of its main attractions. Conversely, the disadvantages of connectivity sharing and a high barrier-to-entry from low initial penetration create strong disincentives to its adoption. The paper's contributions are in formulating and solving a simple model that captures key aspects of UPC adoption, and in articulating guidelines to make it successful. For analytical tractability, the model is arguably simplistic, but the robustness of its findings is demonstrated numerically across a wide range of more general (and more realistic) configurations.

1 Introduction

There is no denying that we are a networked society, and the increasing capabilities and versatility of mobile devices has fueled a growing thirst for ubiquitous connectivity, *i.e.*, connectivity everywhere and all the time. This has driven the growth and success of wireless carriers worldwide. These carriers tout comprehensive coverage and connectivity that in some instances approaches that of wired networks. However, their very success has often made it difficult to maintain the connectivity quality their users expect [19]. This is in part because connectivity relies on a costly *infrastructure,* whose deployment calls for careful long-term planning. This together with the relatively high cost of those services has awaken interest in alternative solutions to offering ubiquitous connectivity.

One such promising alternative is that of *user provided connectivity* (UPC), where connectivity grows "organically" as more users join the network and improve its coverage. In UPC, as users gain (local) access to connectivity, *e.g.*, from subscribing to an Internet Service Provider (ISP), they allow others to share that connectivity in exchange for either compensation or reciprocation. More specifically, a UPC user allows *roaming* users to obtain connectivity through its own local access for a small fee or the ability to enjoy the same benefits when

---

* This work was supported by NSF grant CNS-0915982.

J. Cohen, P. Maillé, and B. Stiller (Eds.): ICQT 2011, LNCS 6995, pp. 38–49, 2011.

itself roaming. This is made possible by the availability of low-cost wire-less access solutions (Wi-Fi), as popularized through services such as FON (http://www.fon.com). FON users purchase an access router (FONERA) that they use for their own local broadband access, but with the agreement that a (small) fraction of their access bandwidth can be made available to other FON users. In exchange, they receive the same privileges when roaming, *i.e.*, they are able to connect through the access points of other FON users.

The challenge faced by such a service model is that while its has low deploy-ment costs (no expensive infrastructure build-out), it does not offer truly ubiq-uitous connectivity until it has reached a large enough level of penetration, *i.e.*, there are enough users to offer comprehensive coverage. This high externality in the service's value can, therefore, hamper early adoption and hence eventual suc-cess. Consider for example a FON-like service starting with no users. This makes the service unattractive to users that value ubiquitous connectivity highly, *e.g.*, users that roam frequently, because the limited coverage offers little connectivity beyond that of a user's "home base". On the other hand, sedentary users are unaffected by the negative utility associated with low coverage, and if the price is low enough can derive positive utility from the service; hence joining. If enough such (sedentary) users join, coverage may increase past a point where it becomes attractive to roaming users who will start joining. This would then ensure rapid growth of the service, were it not for a negative dimension to that growth.

Specifically, as more roaming users join, they start consuming resources in the home bases of other users. This lessens the utility these users derive from the service. This can cause some (sedentary) users to leave, and the corresponding reduction in coverage makes the service less attractive to roaming users that also start leaving. As a result, the initial period of growth in the service is followed by a decline, and the process repeats. The extent to which such behaviors arise depends on many factors, including the benefits users derive from the system, its cost, the severity of the degradations they experience when other users access the network through their home base, and the possible incentives the service provider offers to compensate for those.

The goal of this paper is to develop a simple model that can help understand how these many factors interact and affect the adoption of UPC services. The paper's contributions include

- Identifying service adoption equilibria (or lack thereof) and how they are influenced by system parameters;
- Characterizing "regions" (ranges of price and user valuation) that result in high or low adoption equilibria;
- Validating the robustness of the findings through the numerical evaluation of more realistic (and more complex) models.

The rest of the paper is structured as follows. Section 2 introduces the model and its parameters. Solution methods and findings are presented in Section 3. Section 4 demonstrates the robustness of the results to generalizations of the model. Finally, Section 5 gives a brief overview of related works, while Section 6 summarizes the paper's results and points to possible extensions.

2   Model Formulation

This section introduces a simple model for the decision process of individual users faced with the question of whether to adopt a UPC service. As commonly done, adoption depends on the *utility* a user derives from the service, with users adopting if their utility is non-negative. Utility depends on several factors, including the number (coverage) and type (roaming or not) of existing adopters. Users are myopic when evaluating the utility they expect to derive from the service, *i.e.,* do not account for the impact of their decision on other users, but as adoption levels change, an individual user's utility varies. In other words, the service value exhibit (positive and negative) externalities that affect adoption decisions. It is those dynamics we seek to capture.

For analytical tractability, the model relies on a number of simplifying assumptions. They are relaxed in Section 4, where we show that the findings remain qualitatively unchanged. The utility $U(\theta)$ of a user considering the adoption of a UPC service is given in Eq. (1), where θ, $0 \leq \theta \leq 1$ represents the roaming characteristics of the user, *i.e.,* a low θ indicates a sedentary user while a high θ corresponds to a user that frequently roams. The exact value of θ is private information, but its distribution (over the user population) is known.

$$U(\theta) = \gamma + \theta f(x) - p - g(m) + g^*(m). \tag{1}$$

The parameter γ denotes the intrinsic utility that all users associate with basic home connectivity, while $\theta f(x)$ represents the utility they derive from being able to connect through the home base of other users while roaming. The function $f(x)$ reflects the coverage that the UPC service offers, which grows with the level of adoption x, $0 \leq x \leq 1$. The factor θ in $\theta f(x)$ accounts for the effect of heterogeneity in the roaming characteristics of users, *i.e.,* low θ or sedentary users derive comparatively little benefits from being able to connect through other users' home base. The impact of heterogeneity could arguably be extended to how users value basic connectivity, *i.e.,* γ, as well as capture the fact that roaming users (high θ values) may in turn put less value than sedentary users on home connectivity. The assumption of a fixed γ value across users is a reflection of our focus on understanding how a UPC service can be attractive to users that require more than just home connectivity, *i.e.,* we are not trying to model the adoption of basic Internet service. Conversely, accounting for the fact that roaming users may value home connectivity less could be accomplished by replacing γ by $(1 - \theta)\gamma$. As shown in Appendix A of [1], this does not affect the overall structure of the model. As a result, we only consider the utility function of Eq. (1) in the rest of the paper.

The parameter p is the price charged for the service, while the factors $g(m)$ and $g^*(m)$ capture how roaming traffic affects users, with m measuring the volume of roaming traffic in the system (a function of how many roaming users have joined). Specifically, $-g(m)$ is the (negative) utility associated with roaming traffic consuming resources in the home base of other users. We note that this penalty depends only on the volume of roaming traffic and not on the availability of resources at a user's base station. This is reasonable in the context of home based Internet connectivity where access bandwidth is the main resource, and roaming users can connect at any time. Conversely, the quantity $g^*(m)$ represents possible compensation that the UPC service provider may offer to offset the negative impact of roaming traffic, *e.g.*, by logging external accesses to a user's home base and offering payment for each instance.

For analytical tractability, we make several assumptions regarding the form and range of the parameters of Eq. (1) (as mentioned earlier, Section 4 explores the impact of relaxing many of those assumptions).

First, the parameter θ that measures a user's propensity to roam, is taken to be uniformly distributed in $[0, 1]$. This implies that the adoption level, x, of a UPC service is given by

$$x = \int_0^1 I_{[U(\theta)]} \, d\theta, \qquad (2)$$

where $I_{[U(\theta)]}$ is an indicator function that takes value 1 if $U(\theta) \geq 0$ and zero otherwise.

Next, we assume that the distributions of users over the service area and their roaming patterns are uniform. A uniform distribution of users implies that coverage grows in proportion to adoption, x. Similarly, uniform roaming patterns mean that roaming traffic is evenly distributed across users' home bases, *i.e.*, on average all home bases see the same volume of roaming traffic.

The next assumption concerns the shape of the function $f(x)$. Specifically, we expect frequently roaming users, *i.e.*, users with a high θ value, to see little or no value in the service until its penetration is high enough to realize a certain minimum level of coverage. This means that the overall connectivity utility of those users, as measured by $\gamma + \theta f(x)$, should be positive only once x is large enough. For ease of exposition we use the function $f(x)$ below to capture this effect.

$$f(x) = d\,(2x - 1), \quad d > 0,$$

where the factor d scales the weight of this utility relative to other terms in $U(\theta)$.

The function $f(x)$ is linear in x and negative for small x, *i.e.*, for x below a threshold value of $1/2^1$. It should be noted that a similar outcome could be realized while keeping $f(x)$ positive for all x, by assuming instead that the value of home base connectivity decreases for roaming users, *i.e.*, replace γ by $(1-\theta)\gamma$ in Eq. (1). As discussed in Appendix A of [1], this yields a structurally equivalent model.

With a similar goal of simplicity, both the penalty and the compensation that users receive from providing connectivity to roaming traffic are assumed proportional to the volume of roaming traffic they carry. In other words, the functions $g(m)$ and $g^*(m)$ are taken to be linear functions of m, *i.e.*,

$$g(m) = c\,m, \quad c > 0$$
$$g^*(m) = b\,m, \quad b > 0$$

---

[1] Other threshold values obviously quantitatively affect the outcome, but do not qualitatively affect overall *behaviors*.

where

$$m = \int_0^1 \theta I_{[U(\theta)]}\, d\theta \,.$$

In practice, the volume of roaming traffic at individual home bases varies. However, users whose home base carries more roaming traffic also receive a proportionally larger compensation (when $b > 0$). This should mitigate the impact of heterogeneity.

Using the above assumptions in Eq. (1), a user's utility becomes

$$U(\theta) = k + l\, m + \theta\, (2\, x - 1)\,, \tag{3}$$

where $k = \gamma - p$ and $l = b - c$, and where for normalization purposes, the maximum roaming utility d was taken to be 1. We also assume that roaming and home base connectivity are of a similar nature, so that the utility γ derived from home base connectivity is no more than the maximum utility from roaming connectivity, *i.e.*, $0 \leq \gamma \leq 1$. From the above expression for k, this then implies

$$k \leq 1 - p \leq 1. \tag{4}$$

Before proceeding with investigating the adoption process that Eq. (3) gives rise to, we note that its parameters $k = \gamma - p$ and $l = b - c$ include both *exogenous* and potentially *endogenous* components. Specifically, γ and c capture external system properties, *i.e.*, users valuation for connectivity and their sensitivity to the impact of roaming traffic, respectively. The values of such exogenous parameters can be estimated, *e.g.*, using techniques from marketing research as discussed in [10], but not controlled. In contrast, the service price, p, and incentives for providing connectivity to roaming users, b, are both under the control of the UPC provider. They can, therefore, arguably be endogenized to optimize some measure of success such as profit. Using the results of this paper to explore such options is a topic of ongoing research.

3   Equilibria and Adoption Dynamics

With Eq. (3) in place, it is possible to investigate the dynamics of user adoption over time. We formulate a discrete-time model that evaluates user adoption decisions at successive epochs. For simplicity[2], at epoch $(n + 1)$ all users are assumed to know the system state produced by adoption decisions at epoch n. Users with a non-negative utility then proceed to adopt. Specifically, the utility at epoch $(n + 1)$, $U_{n+1}(\theta)$, of a user with roaming value θ is given by

$$U_{n+1}(\theta) = k + l\, m_n + \theta\, (2\, x_n - 1)\,, \tag{5}$$

where x_n and m_n are the adoption level and volume of roaming traffic produced by adoption decisions at epoch n.

---

[2] Section 4 gives numerical results for a more realistic, diffusion-based adoption model.

The next proposition (the proof is in Appendix B of [1]) establishes a key result that ensures the analytical tractability of a solution, namely, that as the system evolves adopters remain associated with a continuous set of θ values. In other words, the set of adopters does not fragment.

Proposition 1. *For all choices[3] of $k, 0 < k \leq 1$ and l, the set of adopters is characterized by a range of θ values of the form $[0, \widehat{\theta}]$ or $[\widehat{\theta}, 1], 0 \leq \widehat{\theta} \leq 1$.*

Returning to Eq. (5), note that m_n depends not just on the overall adoption level, x_n, but also on *which* users have adopted. This is because the amount of roaming traffic a user contributes depends on its θ value. As a result, characterizing the system state calls for specifying the level of adoption *and* identifying adopters. As shown in Appendix B of [1], adoption at epoch $n + 1$ then depends on adoption levels at *both* epochs n and $n - 1$. Specifically, x_{n+1} depends on x_n, *and* on whether x_{n-1} was in the range $[0, 1/2)$ or $[1/2, 1]$. Although as stated in Proposition 1 adopter sets remain continuous, they can experience abrupt changes when adoption crosses the threshold ($x = 1/2$) of $f(x)$. Abrupt changes are inherent in discrete time models, but as shown in Appendix B of [1], this introduces additional difficulties in characterizing adoption evolution. These are technical in nature, and call for the use of different functional expressions when characterizing adoption after crossing the $x = 1/2$ threshold (in either direction).

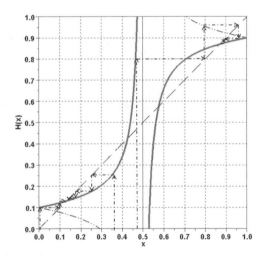

Fig. 1. Adoption Evolution as a Function of Initial Adoption

This is illustrated in Fig. 1, which corresponds to a scenario where depending on initial adoption levels, final adoption can converge to either one of two stable[4] equilibria in $[0, 1/2)$ or $[1/2, 1]$. The x-axis of the figure is the current adoption level, while the y-axis, $H(x)$, denotes the next adoption level given x. The dash-dot curves of Fig. 1 correspond to expressions that characterize the evolution

---

[3] Starting from zero adoption, non-zero adoption is possible only if $k > 0$.

[4] In this scenario, there is also an unstable equilibrium in each of $[0, 1/2)$ and $[1/2, 1]$.

of adoption just after crossing the $x = 1/2$ threshold, while the solid lines are used to characterize adoption while it progresses inside either $[0, 1/2)$ or $[1/2, 1]$. The dashed arrows illustrate adoption trajectories for different initial adoption levels. For example, when the system starts with no adopters, $x_0 = 0$, adoption increases monotonically until it reaches about 10%, the stable equilibrium in $[0, 1/2)$. If seeding is used, $i.e.$, $x_0 > 0$, the outcome depends on the seeding level. When seeding is "low," $e.g.$, $x_0 \approx 35\%$, adoption declines back to 10%. If seeding is high enough, $e.g.$, $x_0 \approx 46\%$, adoption enters $[1/2, 1]$ and eventually converges to the higher adoption equilibrium in that interval (around 85%).

Using the approach developed in Appendix C of [1], adoption evolution can be characterized. Possible outcomes are summarized in the table on the left-hand-side of Fig. 2, with the right-hand-side displaying the regions of the (k, l) plane corresponding to each table entry. Region boundaries, $i.e.$, f_1, f_2, f_3 and f_4, are derived from conditions on the roots of the equation $H(x) = x$ as discussed in Appendix C of [1]. There can be multiple equilibria, both stable (•) and unstable (∘), as well as fixed points associated with an "orbit" (↻). Orbits can be convergent, periodic, or chaotic depending on the choice of (k, l) values (in regions 2' and 3'). Finally, some (k, l) values (region 1) altogether result in the absence of any equilibrium (denoted by — in the table).

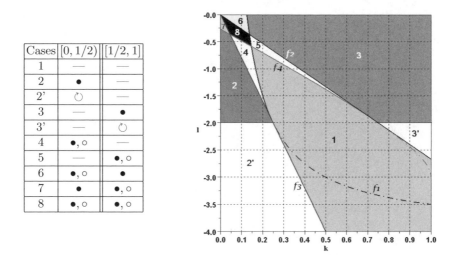

Cases	$[0, 1/2)$	$[1/2, 1]$
1	—	—
2	•	—
2'	↻	—
3	—	•
3'	—	↻
4	•, ∘	—
5	—	•, ∘
6	•, ∘	•
7	•	•, ∘
8	•, ∘	•, ∘

Fig. 2. Possible Combinations of Equilibria and Associated Regions of the (k, l) Plane

The scenario shown in Fig. 1 corresponds to Case 8 of Fig. 2, where as discussed earlier, convergence to a stable equilibrium in either $[0, 1.2)$ or $[1/2, 1]$ is possible depending on initial adoption levels. As indicated in the table of Fig. 2, other behaviors are possible based on which region of the (k, l) plane the system parameters belong to. In the rest of this section, we review the different possible outcomes that can arise, and attempt to provide some intuition in how and why they are associated with different combinations of system parameters.

Behavior (i): Absence of Convergence to an Equilibrium. This arises in Cases $1, 2'$, and $3'$. Region 1 consists of relatively high values of $k(= \gamma - p)$, *i.e.*, at its offered price the intrinsic value of the service is reasonably high, but rather negative values of $l(= b-c)$, *i.e.*, even accounting for compensation (b), the negative impact of roaming traffic is high. This produces the following dynamics: When the service has few users, coverage is low and frequently-roaming users find the service unattractive in spite of the high k. In contrast, sedentary users are unaffected by the limited coverage, and the high k value entices them to adopt. As they adopt, coverage improves and the service becomes attractive to roaming users, which start adopting. The associated growth in roaming traffic, however, starts to negatively affect sedentary users that derive little benefits from the improved coverage. This leads some of them to disadopt, which reduces coverage so that eventually roaming users start leaving as well. Once roaming traffic has been sufficiently reduced, the service becomes again attractive to sedentary users, and the cycle repeats. A similar, albeit more nuanced process is at work in regions $2'$ and $3'$. Appendix C of [1] offers additional discussions.

Behavior (ii): Convergence to a Single Stable Equilibrium in Either $[0, 1/2)$ or $[1/2, 1]$, *independent* **of Initial Adoption.** This arises in Cases 2, 3, 4, and 5. Cases 2 and 4 correspond to low k values and relatively large negative l values. Because of the low k value, few sedentary users adopt and coverage never gets high enough to make the service attractive to frequent roamers. Hence, adoption saturates at a low level in $[0, 1/2)$. Seeding is of no help in this case, as a combination of a low intrinsic value and a high (negative) impact of roaming traffic keeps the service unattractive to frequent roamers even if coverage is artificially increased. A symmetric situation exists in Cases 3 and 5, where adoption converges to a single stable equilibrium in $[1/2, 1]$. The value of k is now relatively high and l boasts only a small negative value. The high intrinsic value of the service initially attracts sedentary users that are not deterred by the limited coverage. Once enough of them have adopted, frequent roamers start joining. Because incentives compensate for the impact of the increasing roaming traffic, few sedentary users leave and adoption stabilizes at a high level.

Behavior (iii): Convergence to One of Two Stable Equilibria in $[0, 1/2)$ or $[1/2, 1]$, as a *function* **of Initial Adoption.** This arises in Cases 6, 7, and 8, which share relatively low k values and marginally negative l values. Under those conditions, while adoption (coverage) is low, frequent roamers are not interested in the service and the small k value limits the number of sedentary users who adopt. Hence, adoption saturates at a low level. However, unlike **(ii)**, this is an instance where seeding can help. In particular, a high enough level of seeding can lead to a much higher final adoption (in $[1/2, 1]$ as opposed to $[0, 1/2)$). Specifically, if seeding is high enough, frequent roamers will start adopting in spite of the low k value. As their number grows and coverage continues improving more adopt and even some sedentary users might also adopt because of the relatively high level of compensation they receive to allow roaming traffic through their home base. As a result, overall adoption eventually stabilizes at a high level.

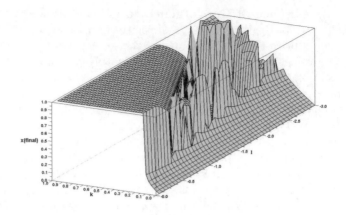

Fig. 3. Adoption Outcomes as a Function of k and l

The above behaviors are illustrated in Fig. 3 that plots the "final" adoption levels for different (k, l) pairs when starting from an initial adoption level of $x_0 = 0$. In scenarios where adoption does not converge, *i.e.*, **Behavior (i)**, the adoption level reported in the figure was sampled at a particular iteration. The figure clearly identifies the regions of the (k, l) plane that correspond to chaotic or at least non-converging adoption (regions $1, 2'$, and $3'$), low adoption (regions 2 and 4, as well as regions 6, 7, and 8 since no seeding was used), and regions of high adoption (regions 3 and 5).

4   Robustness to Model Variations

The model and the analysis behind the paper's results are predicated on a number of simplifying assumptions that are unlikely to hold in practice. It is, therefore, important to validate that the findings and insight derived from these results remain applicable under more realistic conditions. For that purpose, a number of "perturbations" were introduced to the modeling assumptions, and their impact on the results evaluated. The perturbations that were investigated include

1. Relaxing the synchronized nature of adoption decisions and perfect knowledge of system state, *i.e.*, through a "diffusion-like" process that introduces heterogeneity in how users learn and react to changes in system state.
2. Generalizing the distribution of users' roaming characteristics θ, and therefore sensitivity to coverage, *i.e.*, from uniform to arbitrary distributions;
3. Varying users' sensitivity to roaming traffic and incentives compensating for it, *i.e.*, by considering sub-linear and super-linear utility functions;

Because those perturbations typically imply a loss of analytical tractability, numerical evaluations were used to assess their impact. A representative scenario is shown in Fig. 4 that assumes a diffusion-like adoption process in a configuration where the analysis predicts the existence of both a stable and an unstable equilibrium in $[1/2, 1]$. The paper's analytical model assumes that adoption proceeds by discrete jumps, so that it eventually enters a region where convergence to the stable equilibrium is guaranteed. Adoption progression is different under a diffusion-like model, as there is latency in how changes in adoption affect users' utility, and therefore adoption decisions. As a result, adoption trajectories can "traverse" unstable equilibria, but those traversals can depend on the initial service penetration, *e.g.*, as realized through seeding. This is illustrated in Fig. 4.

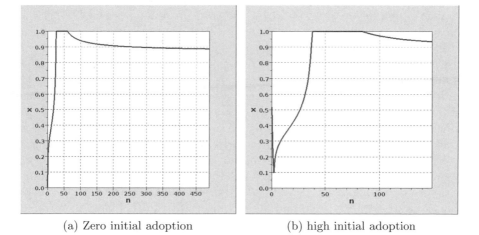

(a) Zero initial adoption   (b) high initial adoption

Fig. 4. Adoption evolution as a function of initial penetration

Fig. 4a illustrates the adoption trajectory when the service starts from zero penetration. In this case, adoption starts relatively steeply as the service is attractive to many sedentary (low θ) users. Adoption then slows down as it approaches the unstable equilibrium, but the initial momentum is sufficient to "carry it through" that region. The pace of adoption then picks up again and eventually overshoots the stable equilibrium before it finally converges back to it. Fig. 4b shows a different behavior when initial penetration is high, *e.g.*, because of seeding, but below the unstable equilibrium. In this scenario, the artificially inflated utility of many adopters drops quickly and they disadopt, which triggers a rapid initial drop in service adoption. However, once adoption has dropped sufficiently, a similar process as that followed in Fig. 4a emerges, and adoption proceeds to grow again and finally converge to the same final adoption level.

Details reporting the outcome of investigations of many other perturbation scenarios can be found in Appendix D of [1]. They establish that the main findings of the paper remain valid in those more general and realistic settings.

5   Related Works

The service adoption process that the paper targets exhibits both positive and negative externalities. There is a vast literature investigating the effect of externalities, often called *network effects* [13], but the majority of these works focus on either positive or negative externalities separately. See for example [4,5,8,11] for works exploring the impact of positive externalities on product adoption and competition. Conversely, the impact of negative externalities, *e.g.*, from congestion, has been extensively investigated in the context of pricing for both communication networks [9,14,16,18] and transportation systems [2,12,15].

Systems that exhibit both positive and negative externalities have been studied mostly in the context of the theory of clubs [17]. Club-like behaviors also arise in peer-to-peer (p2p) systems where more peers increase the total resources available to store content, but induce a higher load on file-serving peers. This has triggered the investigation of *incentives* to promote resources sharing, *e.g.*, BitTorrent "tit-for-tat" [6] or [7] that also explores a possible application to a wireless access system similar in principle to the one considered in this paper.

This paper differs from these earlier works in a number of ways. It introduces a model for individual adoption decisions of a service, which allows for heterogeneity in the users' valuation of the service. In particular, certain users (roaming users) have a strong disincentive to adoption when coverage/penetration is low, while others (sedentary users) are mostly insensitive to this factor. Conversely, this heterogeneity is also present in the negative externality associated with an increase in service adoption, which depends not just on the number of adopters, but on their identity as well, *i.e.*, roaming or sedentary users.

6   Conclusion

The paper introduces a simple model that captures the positive and negative externalities of a UPC service. The model's solution characterizes possible outcomes (equilibria) and when they arise. The robustness of the findings to relaxations in the model's simplifying assumptions was verified numerically.

There are many extensions of interest to this basic model. The first is to endogenize system parameters associated with prices and incentives, based on a revenue maximization objective. This is the topic of ongoing work. Empirical validation of the approach is also obviously desirable and a target for future work, *e.g.*, by collaboration with a UPC provider such as FON. Other extensions include the introduction of competition between UPC and infrastructure based services, as well as the investigation of the possible benefits of cooperation between two such offerings *i.e.*, how a UPC service can best complement a traditional 3G or 4G offering. This is a topic that has seen much recent interest [3] because of the rise in bandwidth demand originating from smartphone and other Internet-enabled portable devices, *e.g.*, e-readers.

References

1. Afrasiabi, M.H., Guérin, R.: Exploring user-provided connectivity – a simple model. Technical report, U. Pennsylvania (2011), http://www.seas.upenn.edu/~afram/tr/upc2011.pdf
2. Beckmann, M., McGuire, C.B., Winsten, C.B.: Studies in the Economics of Transportation. Cowles Commission Monograph. Yale University Press, New Haven (1956)
3. Burstein, D.: 21st Century triple networks: Ubiquitous 4G, WiFi, & Wires. CircleID - Internet Infrastuctur. (January 28, 2011)
4. Cabral, L.: On the adoption of innovation with network externalities. Mathematical Social Sciences 19 (1990)
5. Choi, J.P.: The provision of (two-way) converters in the transition process to a new incompatible technology. The Journal of Industrial Economics 45(2) (1997)
6. Cohen, B.: Incentives build robustness in BitTorrent. In: Proc. 1st Workshop Econ. Peer-to-Peer Sys, Berkeley, CA (June 2003)
7. Courcoubetis, C., Weber, R.: Incentives for large peer-to-peer systems. J. Select. Areas. Commun. 24(5) (May 2006)
8. Farrell, J., Saloner, G.: Installed base and compatibility: Innovation, product pre-announcements, and predation. American Economic Review 76 (1986)
9. Gibbens, R.J., Kelly, F.P.: Resource pricing and the evolution of congestion control. Automatica 35 (1999)
10. Green, P.E., Krieger, A., Wind, Y.: Thirty years of conjoint analysis: Reflections and prospects. Interfaces 31(3), S56–S73 (2001)
11. Katz, M., Shapiro, C.: Technology adoption in the presence of network externalities. Joural of Political Economy 94(3) (June 1986)
12. Kelly, F.P.: Road pricing. Ingenia 29 (2006)
13. Liebowitz, S., Margolis, S.: Network effects. In: Cave, M., Majumdar, S., Vogelsang, I. (eds.) Handbook of Telecommun. Econ., vol. 1, Elsevier, Amsterdam (2002)
14. MacKie-Mason, J.K., Varian, H.R.: Pricing the internet. Computational Economics 9401002, EconWPA (January 1994)
15. Odlyzko, A.: The evolution of price discrimination in transportation and its implications for the Internet. Review of Network Economics 3 (2004)
16. Paschalidis, I.C., Tsitsiklis, J.N.: Congestion-dependent pricing of network services. IEEE/ACM Transactions on Networking 8(2) (April 2000)
17. Sandler, T., Tschirhart, J.T.: The economic theory of clubs: An evaluative survey. Journal of Economic Literature 18(4) (December 1980)
18. Srikant, R.: The Mathematics of Internet Congestion Control. Birkhäuser, Basel (2004)
19. Wortham, J.: Customers angered as iPhones overload AT&T. The New York Times (September 2, 2009)

Network Bandwidth Allocation with End-to-End QoS Constraints and Revenue Sharing in Multi-domain Federations

Isabel Amigo[1,2], Pablo Belzarena[1], Federico Larroca[1], and Sandrine Vaton[2]

[1] Facultad de Ingeniería, Universidad de la República, Montevideo, Uruguay
[2] Telecom Bretagne, Brest, France

Abstract. Internet is evolving, traffic continues to grow, new revenue sources are sought by Network and Service Providers. Value added services with real time characteristics are likely to be common currency in the near future. Quality of Service (QoS) could allow Application/Service Providers (APs) to offer better services to the end users. At the same time, all actors claim for a fair distribution of revenues. Inspired by this scenario, we propose a complete framework for selling interdomain quality assured services, and subsequently distributing revenues, in an Autonomous System (AS) association context. We state the problem as a network utility maximization problem with QoS constraints and show that a distributed solution can be carried out. In order to fairly share the resulting revenue we study concepts from coalitional game theory and propose a solution based on the Shapley value and statistics on the revenues. Simulations of the whole proposal are shown.

Keywords: Auctions, QoS, Shapley Value.

1 Introduction

Internet traffic is likely to continue increasing in a non-stop fashion. Recent studies [2] show that not only the tendency is to increase in amount but in quality requirements as well, since the applications which are envisioned to have the greatest increase are those with real time characteristics.

Nowadays, the focus of telecommunication market is on best effort content and in order to meet customer expectations telecommunications companies are forced to invest in capacity, without getting sufficient return on these investments to have sustainable businesses. The ever evolving features provided by the handset terminals, and the growing number of connection capable equipments, constitute more evidence in favor of the forecast of Internet traffic increase.

Moreover, emerging technologies such as telepresence or cloud computing not only generate large volumes of traffic with real time requirements, but are also used to interconnect sites around the globe. As a consequence, in addition to a QoS capable network, this kind of services require an end-to-end QoS enabled chain crossing heterogeneous carrier networks [15].

J. Cohen, P. Maillé, and B. Stiller (Eds.): ICQT 2011, LNCS 6995, pp. 50–62, 2011.
© Springer-Verlag Berlin Heidelberg 2011

In this scenario, nowadays Internet business rules for domain interconnection may not be able to provide a sustainable economy for all actors in the value chain (Application Providers, Network Service Providers, etc.). Indeed, these rules (peering agreements) are not aware of the QoS capabilities of the domains and most of them are based on a traffic-symmetry premise that may no longer be valid in evolving services (for instance HD video on demand). Moreover, a common way of pricing for Internet connection is a monthly flat rate, while other actors, e.g. APs or the so-called Over the Top Providers (OTTs) receive revenues on a per bandwidth-consumed basis, relying their services on the existent network infrastructure but not remunerating Network Providers adequately [11].

Taking into account the previous considerations many companies and academic groups are analyzing future scenarios so as to meet the end-to-end requirements and business models. As a possible architecture to provide these services, the ASs alliances or federations have emerged (see for instance [1]). In this kind of interconnection market there exists a cooperation on infrastructure, policies and incentives for rational usage of resources and agreements for providing end-to-end QoS. At the same time, interesting issues arise, such as priorities and revenue sharing. In this work, we aim at providing a framework in that sense.

We shall focus on a scenario in which ASs work together in a collaborative way in order to sell end-to-end quality assured bit pipes. The pipes are not necessarily sold to the final user but are rather sold to intermediate actors like brokers or OTT which will in turn resell them to the final user, by providing their own services through a quality assured path.

In this context, our contribution is actually twofold. On the one hand, we address the bandwidth allocation problem providing a solution through which the end-to-end quality parameters are assured and the revenue of the whole alliance is maximized. In addition, we prove that this mechanism can be carried out on a distributed fashion. On the other hand, we cover a subsequent problem that is how to distribute the revenues among all the members of the alliance. In this regard, we provide a mechanism that has fairness properties and provides incentives to the ASs to increase their features towards the federation. Beyond the specific contributions, the proposed framework links the revenue income mechanism with the revenue sharing one, which to the best of our knowledge has not been proposed in this context before.

2   Bandwidth Allocation with End-to-End QoS Constraints

We are interested, as aforementioned, on a scenario where several ASs work together to sell capacity on a multidomain quality assured path. We shall refer to the quality assured path as *QoS pipe* or as *path*.

In this scenario, the capacity dedicated by each AS to sell by this means is a portion of their already deployed capacity. That is to say, ASs have their infrastructure through which traditional services are sold following the best-effort paradigm and they decide to dedicate some portion of their capacity to the federation.

For each QoS pipe there is a group of users or buyers interested on getting a portion of bandwidth on that pipe. The amount of money this group is willing to pay for each value of bandwidth is the so-called utility function. The objective is to sell the available resources in such a way that the revenue of the whole alliance is maximized while the end-to-end constraints are accomplished. We shall work with the end-to-end delay.

Let us introduce some notations so as to formally represent the scenario described above. Each AS in the alliance is abstracted to a node indexed by n with an equivalent capacity of c_n. The complete set of nodes is denoted by N. More complex topology abstrction models could be used instead of the single node aggregation. Though we leave out of the scope of this work the study of the AS topology abstraction, other alternatives and more comments can be seen in [3]. The available pipes are the ones in the set S and are indexed by s. The constraint on the delay on path s (i.e. the maximum admissible delay) is denoted by D_s. We assume that the routes within the alliance are fixed and single-path. We represent these routes with the $|N| \times |S|$ matrix R, where the notation $|\cdot|$ refers to the cardinal of the set. The entry $R_{i,j}$ is equal to 1 if the route of the pipe j traverses the node i and is equal to zero otherwise. We denote pipe's s route as $r(s)$. The bandwidth allocated to pipe s (i.e. the amount of traffic sold to the buyers associated to path s) is denoted by a_s. The utility function associated to each path s is called $U_s(a_s)$. We assume that $U_s(a_s)$ is known and, as usual in this context, it is a strictly concave function of the bandwidth.

Please note that the QoS pipes are defined by an ingress and egress point along with a maximum delay. This implies that two QoS pipes are considered different even if they share exactly the same physical path but provide different delay bounds.

Let us now state some additional assumptions. The delay introduced by each node in a path is an increasing convex function of the bandwidth carried by all the paths traversing the node. We assume that this function can be somehow learned or estimated by the domain, and we leave out of the scope of this paper the means for computing it. The delay function of node n is denoted as $f_n(a)$ where $a = \{a_s\}_{s \in S}$.

The amount of traffic sold to all paths must be such that the revenue perceived by the alliance is maximized while the QoS constraints are fulfilled. This is formalized in the following bandwidth allocation problem:

Problem 1

$$\max_{a_s} \sum_{s:s \in S} U_s(a_s)$$

$$s.t. \sum_{n:n \in r(s)} f_n(a) \leq D_s, \forall s \in S.$$

Remark 1. In Prob. 1 we have not included a capacity constraint which is assumed to be taken into account in f_n. Indeed, if f_n is a barrier function (i.e.

it approaches infinity as the bandwidth approaches the capacity) we can safely ignore any capacity constraint.

Remark 2. The fact that the association may not want to sell bandwidth on a certain path if the incomes perceived by doing so are lower than a certain bound is not considered either. However, we can model this situation by defining a cost function of the allocated bandwidth $\kappa_s(a_s)$ for each service $s \in S$ and modifying the objective function in Prob. 1 by $\sum_{s \in S} [U_s(a_s) - \kappa_s(a_s)]$. Provided the cost function is convex, the new problem would be analogous to Prob. 1. For the sake of notations simplicity we shall not consider the cost function hereafter.

We aim at solving Prob. 1 in a distributed way. Hence, we shall explore a primal-dual approach for Prob. 1, whose associated Lagrangian is:

$$L(a, \lambda) = \sum_{s:s \in S} \left[U_s(a_s) + \lambda_s \cdot \left(D_s - \sum_{n:n \in r(s)} f_n(a) \right) \right], \tag{1}$$

where $\lambda = \{\lambda_s\}_{s \in S}$ is the vector of Lagrange multipliers.
    To find a saddle point of (1) (i.e. the optimum of Prob. 1) we use the gradient-projection algorithm updating the primal and dual variables as follows:

$$a_s^{t+1} = \left[a_s + \gamma_s \left(U_s'(a_s) - \sum_{n:n \in r(s)} \sum_{v:n \in r(v)} \lambda_v f_n'(a) \right) \right]^+ \tag{2}$$

$$\lambda_s^{t+1} = \left[\lambda_s - \alpha_s \left(D_s - \sum_{n:n \in r(s)} f_n(a) \right) \right]^+ \tag{3}$$

where $[\cdot]^+ = \max\{0, \cdot\}$ and α_s, γ_s are step sizes.
    The updates (2,3) are performed iteratively on each edge router of a pipe, which we call the *source*. Every source sends an initial value for λ_s and a_s through route $r(s)$. Each node receives all the values and computes the delay, the derivative of the delay times the sum of the lambdas it has received and sends them to the source. All these values can be accumulated in two sums in the way back to the source, thus only two values are needed to be sent back to the source on each iteration. Once the source receives such values it proceeds to update the value in λ_s and in a_s. This is repeated iteratively in the control plane and it is run prior to any resource allocation.
    The following theorem proves the convergence of the algorithm.

Theorem 1. *Convergence of the primal-dual algorithm. Given the Prob. 1 let* $\sum_s U_s(a_s)$ *be a strictly concave function and* $f_n(a) \forall n \in N$ *convex functions. Then the iterations* $a_s^t \forall s \in S$ *as defined in* (2) *and* (3) *converge asymptotically to the solution of Prob. 1.*

The proof is not provided here for lack of space reasons. Please refer to [3] for more details.

2.1   Application: Multidomain Network Auctions

We now discuss an example that fits to the model proposed before. We associate to each pipe a service to be sold which has a certain bandwidth σ_s and an assured delay D_s (for instance, this service can be a VoD movie). Several instances of a service are sold through the same pipe.

These services are sold by means of network bandwidth auctions. In particular, we shall follow the first price auctions model where the winner user is charged with the amount he/she bids. This bidding mechanism is the most suitable to our problem as explained in Sect. 5.

We shall first consider the case of one-shot bandwidth auctions. That is to say, that the whole capacity available for providing the services is going to be auctioned at a certain moment.

Let us introduce some new notations. For each service s there are N_s buyers or users, which participate in the auction for obtaining an instance of the service. Each of the N_s users bids $b_s^{(i)}$ which we order as

$$b_s^{(1)} \geq b_s^{(2)} \geq \cdots \geq b_s^{(N_s)}. \tag{4}$$

The resource allocation decision is to find which of these bids to accept, so as to maximize the profit of the whole alliance while the per-route delay remains smaller than a given bound, under a first-price auction. Since for each s all bids are for the same bandwidth and delay constraint, the optimal solution is accepting the highest bids per service. We define the variable $\psi_{s,i}$ which is equal to 1 if bid i for service s is accepted, and zero otherwise. Then, defining the variable m_s as the number of bids accepted for service s we have the following equality:

$$\sum_{i=1}^{N_s} b_s^{(i)} \psi_{s,i} = \sum_{i=1}^{m_s} b_s^{(i)}. \tag{5}$$

Accepting m_s bids would render a total accepted rate of a_s where $a_s = \sigma_s m_s$. Thus, the utility per service can be defined as a function of a_s as

$$U_s(a_s) = \sum_{i=1}^{a_s/\sigma_s} b_s^{(i)}. \tag{6}$$

Equation (6) is defined for discrete values of a_s (the multiples of σ_s). We extend it to a piecewise linear concave function of a_s by linear interpolation.

Altogether, we can write the optimization problem as follows:

Problem 2

$$\max_{a_s} \sum_{s \in S} U_s(a_s)$$

$$s.t. \sum_{n:n \in r(s)} f_n(a) \leq D_s, \, \forall s \in S, \, a_s/\sigma_s \in \mathbb{Z}.$$

In Prob. 2 the objective function is concave but not strictly concave (as in Prob. 1) and an integer restriction has been added. Since integer programming is NP hard, we have strong indication of the difficulty of this problem, not easy to overcome even allowing for centralized computation. We will thus accept a suboptimal allocation which involves solving the convex relaxation, and rounding off to satisfy the integer constraints.

The not strictly concaveness of the utility function may compromise the convergence of the algorithm by producing, in some cases, a hopping result between two consecutive integer values. In order to avoid oscillations we shall use, as proposed in [10], the so-called proximal optimization method which implies modifying the optimization problem by an equivalent one so as to have an strictly concave function as objective without changing the point at which the solution is attained. For lack of space reasons we do not provide further detail on such method.

For selling the services we repeat the process described above in a periodic fashion. Every period of time T, bids are collected and bandwidth is allocated. Most previous work on multi-period auctions (e.g. [8]) allow future bidders to compete with incumbent ones, albeit given the latter some advantage [17]. A different approach (e.g. [4]) is to impose the condition that once bandwidth has been allocated in an auction, the successful bidder has a reservation for the duration of his/her connection. Is out of the scope of this paper the specific solution for multi-period auctions problem and any of the previous proposals can be adopted.

2.2   Simulations

We present an illustrative example of the one-shot allocation mechanism. Consider the Fig. 1(a), where four ASs associate to provide two services. The equivalent capacities of all the ASs are equal to 40. Service 1 (plain path) has a delay bound $D_1 = 2$ while service 2 (dashed path) provides a delay bound $D_2 = 0.5$. Both services offer an amount of bandwidth of 8. All values are expressed in a certain coherent unit. For both services 10 buyers offer their bids. In Fig. 1(b) the resulting utility function for each service is shown. In this case the service with the most constrictive delay bound has received higher bids. Figure 1(c) shows the evolution of the rate for each service throughout the iterations needed for the convergence of the distributed algorithm. Results show that the service which implies more incomes is the one that gets more rate accepted. Figure 1(e) shows the evolution of the delays and that both constraints are accomplished. Finally, Fig. 1(d) shows the evolution of the revenue perceived per service.

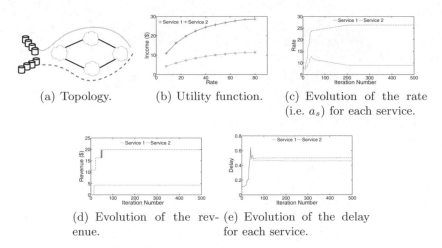

(a) Topology.   (b) Utility function.   (c) Evolution of the rate (i.e. a_s) for each service.

(d) Evolution of the rev-   (e) Evolution of the delay
enue.   for each service.

Fig. 1. Bandwidth auctions with QoS constraints, one-shot allocation. Simulations.

3   Revenue Sharing

As we have claimed in Sect. 1, traditional peer paying in the Internet may not be suitable for these kinds of assured quality services. We aim at performing the revenue sharing based on some fairness principles. Idelay, the revenue perceived by each AS should be proportional to the profit it provides to the federation. Moreover, the AS who is responsible for the end-to-end QoS degradation or bottleneck, or somehow limits incomes, should be encouraged to increase the resources dedicated to the alliance. In the following subsection we shall explore the concepts of coalitional game theory as a means of achieving the objectives mentioned above.

3.1   The Shapley Value

The Shapley value, proposed by Lloyd Shapley in 1952 [19], provides a means for performing the revenue sharing of an association or coalition. It has been widely used in the literature for its good properties. We now briefly recall some related concepts. The interested reader is referred to [20] for a complete review on Coalitional Game Theory.

A Coalitional Game with Transferable Utility is a pair (M, v) where M is a finite set of players and $v : 2^M \to \mathbb{R}$, the worth function which associates with each coalition $Q \subseteq M$ a real-valued payoff $v(Q)$ that the members can distribute among them.

Given a game $G = (M, v)$, we shall call $x = \{x_i\}_{\forall i \in M}$ the payoff vector, where x_i represents the share of the grand coalition's (i.e. M) payoff that player $i \in M$ receives. A Pre-imputation is the set of payoff vectors such that the sum of all x_i is equal to $v(M)$. A Dummy player is a player whose contribution to the coalition is the same as the one he/she would achieve on his/her own. With these definitions the axioms of Symmetry (for any v if i and j contribute the same to any coalition then $x_i = x_j$), Dummy player (for any v if i is a dummy player then $x_i = v(\{i\})$) and Additivity are introduced, and the Shapley value is defined as follows.

Theorem 2. *Shapley Value [19]. Given a coalitional game (M, v) there is a unique pre-imputation $\phi(M, v)$ that satisfies the symmetry, dummy player and additivity axioms and it is called the Shapley Value. It is defined, for player i as:*

$$\phi_i(M, v) = \frac{1}{|M|!} \sum_{Q \subseteq M \setminus \{i\}} |Q|!(|M| - |Q| - 1)! \left[v(Q \cup \{i\}) - v(Q) \right].$$

In addition to the properties stated on Theorem 2, the Shapley Value is efficient (it shares the total revenue) and fair. Fairness is defined in terms that for any two players $i, j \in M$, i's contribution to j is equal to j's contribution to i, that is $\phi_i(M, v) - \phi_i(M \setminus \{j\}, v) = \phi_j(M, v) - \phi_j(M \setminus \{i\}, v)$. We shall explore in the following subsection if it incentives the AS to provide better resources towards the association.

3.2   Combining the Shapley Value and the Mean Utility

In order to share the incomes perceived by means of the mechanism introduced in Sect. 2 we propose to manage two time scales. One timescale, say hourly, in which the bandwidth allocation is performed and revenue is collected. A long one, say monthly, in which the collected revenue is shared among all the ASs of the alliance. This allows for adapting the mechanism to a dynamic approach in which allocations are performed online and decentralized, and a centralized stage in which the revenue sharing is computed offline.

We define a game where the players are the set N of ASs in the association and the worth function is defined as follows. We introduce the assumption that the bids are drawn independently from a continuous probability distribution for each service. Provided this, we can safely represent the utility function of several auctions occurred during a certain period of time by the mean of all the utilities of that period. Thus, we define

$$\overline{U}_s(a_s) = E[U_s(a_s)], \tag{7}$$

which is still a strictly concave function of a_s in the general case, or a piecewise linear concave function in the case introduced in Subsect. 2.1.

In addition, we assume that the delay function of every AS (i.e. f_n) remains unchanged during the considered time period.

Finally, the worth function v is defined for each sub-coalition $Q \subseteq N$ as the solution to Prob. 3, defined as:

Problem 3

$$\max_{a_s} \sum_{s \in S^Q} \overline{U}_s(a_s)$$

$$s.t. \sum_{n:n \in r(s)} f_n(a) \leq D_s, \forall s \in S^Q,$$

where $S^Q \subseteq S$ is the set of services that can be provided by Q.

Once the revenue is collected, during several phases of bandwidth allocation, it is shared among all ASs proportional to the Shapley value. That is to say, we compute $v(Q) \forall Q \subseteq N$ according to Prob. 3 and with these values we compute the Shapley value $\phi_n \forall n \in N$. Finally, node's i revenue is computed as $\Phi_i = \phi_i \times V / \sum_{j \in n}(\phi_j)$, where V is the total revenue perceived by the coalition on the considered period.

We claim that the proposed mechanism provides incentives for the ASs in the association to improve their features towards it. The features we are interested in are the ones that constitute constraints to the incomes (i.e. to Prob. 1). These features are thus captured in the node's delay function (i.e. f_n) and we refer to them as an equivalent capacity for each AS. In the remainder of this section we formalize this property.

Theorem 3. *Incentive for improving capacities. Let (N, v, c) be a coalitional game where the set of nodes N are the players, c represents the equivalent capacities of the nodes in N and v is the worth function defined by Prob. 3. If $i \in N$ increases its capacity then its sharing coefficient (i.e. ϕ_i) will be not decreased. That is, letting c^* represent the capacities of the nodes where i's capacity is increased, $\phi_i(N, v, c*) \geq \phi_i(N, v, c)$, where $\phi_i(N, v, c)$ is the Shapley value of node i given the game (N, v) and the capacities c.*

Proof. By definition of Shapley value $\phi_i(N, v, c*) = \frac{K}{N!} \sum_{Q \subseteq N \setminus \{i\}} [v(Q \cup \{i\}, c^*) - v(Q, c^*)]$, where K is a constant and $v(Q, c^*)$ represents the worth function for subcoalition Q when the capacities are given by c^*.

$$\phi_i(N, v, c*) = \frac{K}{N!} \sum_{Q \subseteq N \setminus \{i\}} [v(Q \cup \{i\}, c^*) - v(Q, c)],$$

holds since the worth function of any coalition without i is the same, regardless the capacity of i. By subtracting i's share coefficient with and without increasing its capacity we have:

$$\phi_i(N, v, c*) - \phi_i(N, v, c) = \frac{K}{N!} \sum_{Q \subseteq N \setminus \{i\}} [v(Q \cup \{i\}, c^*) - v(Q \cup \{i\}, c)].$$

We now determine if the inequality $v(Q \cup \{i\}, c^*) \geq v(Q \cup \{i\}, c) \forall Q \subseteq N$ holds. Indeed, v is the solution to Prob. 3 which is the maximization of a concave function with convex constraints. By increasing the capacity we relax such problem, thus doing so yields to greater or equal solutions. □

Theorem 3 proves that if node i increases its capacity its sharing coefficient increases as well or remains the same. It is now left to be proved that the total revenue perceived by the federation in the considered period (i.e. V) does not decrease either (recall $\Phi_i = \phi_i \times V/\sum_{j \in n}(\phi_j)$). Indeed, if node's i capacity is increased either the association can allocate more bandwidth (and revenue increases) either it can allocate the same amount of bandwidth (and revenue remains the same). An argument similar to the one used before can be used to formalize this reasoning, but now considering Prob. 1 instead of Prob. 3.

3.3 Simulations

We illustrate the proposed method via a simulation with a simple example. Consider the topology shown in Fig. 2(a), where the capacities of the three ASs and their delay functions are the same. Buyers' bids are random. Results of the accumulated revenue for each AS can be seen in Fig. 2(b) represented with thin lines.

In order to explore the influence of the available capacity on the revenue sharing, we consider the topology in Fig. 2(a) but now the equivalent capacity of the shaded node is increased. The cumulative revenue sharing is shown for each AS in Fig. 2(b) in thick lines, we can see that the revenue of the AS that increases its capacity perceives an improvement.

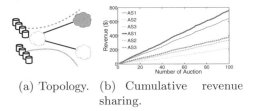

(a) Topology. (b) Cumulative revenue sharing.

Fig. 2. Incentive for increasing capacity towards the federation. Simulation.

4 Implementation Considerations

The multidomain scenario poses new problems that are not experienced in the context of the intradomain one. For instance, political aspects (confidentiality, trust), technical aspects (interoperability, scalability) and economical ones (revenue sharing). We now briefly comment on them.

In the AS Federation context, it is usually considered that the ASs tell the truth and fulfill their common interests. Nevertheless, the ASs in the federations may ask for confidentiality, privacy on committed agreements and freedom on pricing [16].

In the distributed stage, the delay of traversing the AS and its derivative are passed from one AS to another. In the centralized stage, all the ASs in the federation send their delay function and the mean utility function to a centralized trusted entity. Thus, this framework preserves confidentiality.

Pricing can be freely defined at the per service level for the premium services, and at a per AS level for best-effort traffic.

Finally, the proposed solution appears to scale well. For the rate allocation, a few bytes in the forward and backward direction are needed during a preallocation iteration phase. For the revenue sharing, the ASs need to send reduced information to the centralized entity. The computation of the Shapley value is often #P-complete [6]. However, in our working context, the associations would rarely consist of more than ten ASs. For instance, the average AS path in the Internet is of four ASs [7]. In addition, the computation is proposed to be performed offline.

5   Related Work

The topics discussed on this paper are covered in several articles, of which we shall mention only a few of them.

Several works in the literature have proposed bandwidth network auctions for solving the bandwidth allocation problem. Most of them seek bids' truth reveling mechanisms. For instance, the ones based on Vickrey's second price auctions (e.g. [5]) where the winning user is charged the second highest bid, or the ones based on Vickrey-Clark-Groves (VCG) mechanisms (e.g. [5]) as in [8,9,12,17]. Most of these mechanisms need for centralized computation, some of them assume certain network topology while others assume the buyer knows the network topology. In these cases the objective is welfare maximization. Other proposals (e.g. [4]) work with first price auctions. In this kind of auction, revenue maximization is sought and the implementation complexity is much lower than the one present in second price auctions. Moreover, in [13] it is shown that VCG mechanisms can hardly be applied on multidomain networks.

For the reasons exposed above, our auctions proposal is aligned with the one in [4]. However, we consider a multidomain federation scenario rather than a single domain and we incorporate an end-to-end QoS constraint rather than only considering capacity constraints. With respect to this last aspect [18] states a similar problem, but its context and the way it is solved differ significantly from ours.

Regarding revenue sharing, for instance, in [11] the proposal is to change the Internet economics by business contracts whose payment is determined by the Shapley value. In [21,14] the aim is to optimize routing within an alliance of ASs and revenue is shared by means of Shapley value. We share with them the choice of using the Shapley value. However, our proposal incorporates the sell of premium services which are the sources of the revenue, and links the Shapley value with it. In addition, our approach also takes into account the features the ASs provide to the alliance rather that only considering the routing.

6   Conclusion and Future Work

We have proposed a framework for covering the complete cycle for selling end-to-end quality assured services in the context of AS federations. We have stated the problem of network bandwidth allocation with QoS constraints and showed a distributed solution. An application based on network bandwidth auctions for using such problem as the means for selling quality assured paths was shown. A mechanism for performing the revenue sharing of the federation, based on the Shapley value and the mean utility function was proposed. Such mechanism has fairness properties and was proven to incentivize ASs to increase its capacities. The behavior of the whole solution was studied through simulations.

In future work we shall enhance the interdomain network model and deepen on the delay function. In addition, we shall continue the research on revenue sharing, seeking for more properties such as the ones involving the stability of the federations and incentives to collaborate.

Acknowledgment. This work was funded by the ETICS project (EC FP7 248567), cf. www.ict-etics.eu and the Uruguayan Agency for Research and Innovation (ANII) (PR-POS-2008-003 and FCE 2158).

References

1. ETICS: Economics and Technologies for Inter-carrier Services. European research project, supported by the 7th Framework Programme of the European Union, http://www.ict-etics.eu
2. Cisco Systems: Hyperconnectivity and the Approaching Zettabyte Era. Tech. rep (June 2010)
3. Amigo, I., Belzarena, P., Larroca, F., Vaton, S.: Network Bandwidth allocation with end-to-end QoS constraints and Revenue Sharing in Multidomain Federations. Internal Report. Tech. rep. (2011), http://iie.fing.edu.uy/publicaciones/2011/ABLV11/
4. Belzarena, P., Ferragut, A., Paganini, F.: Bandwidth Allocation via Distributed Auctions with Time Reservations. In: Procedings of IEEE INFOCOM, Rio de Janeiro, Brazil (2009)
5. Courcoubetis, C., Weber, R.: Pricing and Communications Networks. John Wiley & Sons, Ltd., Chichester (2003)
6. Deng, X., Papadimitriou, C.H.: On the complexity of cooperative solution concepts. Math. Oper. Res. 19, 257–266 (1994)
7. Dhamdhere, A., Dovrolis, C.: Ten years in the evolution of the internet ecosystem. In: Proceedings of the 8th ACM SIGCOMM, pp. 183–196. ACM, New York (2008)
8. Dramitinos, M., Stamoulis, G.D., Courcoubetis, C.: An auction mechanism for allocating the bandwidth of networks to their users. Comput. Netw. 51, 4979–4996 (2007)
9. Lazar, A.A., Semret, N.: Design and Analysis of the Progressive Second Price Auction for Network Bandwidth Sharing (1999)
10. Lin, X., Shroff, N.B.: Utility Maximization for Communication Networks With Multipath Routing. IEEE Transactions on Automatic Control 51(5), 766–781 (2006)
11. Ma, R.T.B., Chiu, D.M., Lui, J.C.S., Misra, V., Rubenstein, D.: Internet Economics: The Use of Shapley Value for ISP Settlement. IEEE/ACM Transactions on Networking 18(3), 775–787 (2010)

12. Maillé, P., Tuffin, B.: Pricing the internet with multibid auctions. IEEE/ACM Trans. Netw. 14, 992–1004 (2006)
13. Maillé, P., Tuffin, B.: Why VCG auctions can hardly be applied to the pricing of inter-domain and ad hoc networks. In: 3rd EuroNGI Conference, Trondheim, Norway, pp. 36–39 (2007)
14. Mycek, M., Secci, S., Pioro, M., Rougier, J.L., Tomaszewski, A., Pattavina, A.: Cooperative multi-provider routing optimization and income distribution. In: DRCN 2009, pp. 281–288 (October 2009)
15. Le Sauze, N., et al.: ETICS: QoS-enabled interconnection for Future Internet services. In: Future Network and Mobile Summit (2010)
16. Pouyllau, H., Douville, R.: End-to-end QoS negotiation in network federations. In: IEEE/IFIP Network Operations and Management Symposium Workshops (NOMS Wksps), pp. 173–176 (2010)
17. Reichl, P., Bessler, S., Stiller, B.: Second-chance auctions for multimedia session pricing. In: Proc. MIPS 2003 (2003)
18. Saad, M., Leon-garcia, A., Yu, W.: Rate Allocation under Network End-to-End Quality-of-Service Requirements. In: GLOBECOM (2006)
19. Shapley, L.: A value for n-person games. In: Kuhn, H., Tucker, A. (eds.) Contributions to the Theory of Games
20. Shoham, Y., Leyton-Brown, K.: Multiagent Systems: Algorithmic, Game-Theoretic, and Logical Foundations. Cambridge University Press, Cambridge (2009)
21. Secci, S., Rougier, J.-L., et al.: Connection-oriented Service Management in Provider Alliances: a Shapley Value Perspective. In: EuroNF 5th Int. Workshop on Traffic Management and Engineering for the Future Internet (2009)

On the Quantification of Value Networks: A Dependency Model for Interconnection Scenarios*

Patrick Zwickl[1], Peter Reichl[1,2], and Antonio Ghezzi[3]

[1] FTW Telecommunications Research Center Vienna, Austria
{zwickl,reichl}@ftw.at
[2] Université Européenne de Bretagne, Rennes, France
[3] Politecnico di Milano, Department of Management, Economics and Industrial Engineering, Milan, Italy
antonio1.ghezzi@polimi.it

Abstract. Caused by the non-linearity of some industries such as networking interconnection, the deep understanding of Value Networks has grown in importance. While related works such as Value Network Analysis have been subject to the available qualitative mechanisms, this papers aims at quantifying actor dependencies within Value Networks. To this end, a series of dependency indicators are proposed based on well-established economic principles like Porter's Five Forces on firms. This approach is validated through a case study analysing the replaceability of Transit Network Service Providers. Finally, an outlook on bargaining strategies based on these dependency indicators is given.

Keywords: Value Networks, Quantification, Dependency Analysis, Interconnection.

1 Introduction

The emergence of Value Networks (VN) is related to industries with a non-linear value creation, i.e. parallelised business relationship for providing a specific service or good to customers. Thus, classic value chain concepts [1] envisaging the development of value through a series of chained processes may not be significant or even be obsolete for these industries. The networking interconnection (IC) is especially an interesting example. Triggered by this economic interest, a wide range of literature on VN's principles (external view of enterprises—the business relationships of firms) is available—e.g. [2], [3], [4], or [5]—whose understanding has to be set in relationship to business models (internal perspective of an enterprise)—e.g. [6], or [7].

---

* The research leading to these results has received funding from the European Community's Seventh Framework Programme (FP7/2007-2013) under grant agreement n°248567 for the ETICS project. Further information is available at www.ict-etics.eu. P. Reichl would like to acknowledge additional funding from Université Européenne de Bretagne in the framework of the SISCom International Research Chair on "Future Telecommunication Ecosystems".

J. Cohen, P. Maillé, and B. Stiller (Eds.): ICQT 2011, LNCS 6995, pp. 63–74, 2011.

The need of understanding the fundamentals about particular VNs has yielded the proposition of Value Network Analysis (VNA) [8]—a concept for qualitatively analysing VNs[1] such as discussed for tangible and intangible assets in [9], e.g. for identifying misspecification, inefficient value flows, role interdependencies, response-delivery relationships, risks, analysis on tangible and intangible deliveries and heart beat roles of the VNs. Unfortunately, actors' dependencies on the VN, or quantified VN representations have not yet emerged, which may aggravate precise analysis and optimisation of VNs' natures. Thus, essential research questions in the IC business—like the role and/or replaceability of Transit Network Service Provider (*NSP*)—cannot be resolved by quantified answers.

Therefore, in this paper we present an approach for deriving quantitative metrics (dependency indicators) for VNs based on VNA concepts. To this end, in Section 2.2 we review related fundamental economic approaches, i.e. Porter's five forces on firms [10] and Value Models, which are in turn integrated into a Value Network Dependency Model (*VNDM*). Based on these considerations, a series of relative dependency indicators for actor entities are established in Section 3, which model the degree of dependency of an entity on a VN. In Section 4, a case study investigates the replaceability of Transit NSPs for a global Video on Demand stream example, and demonstrates how this approach provides proper tools for analysing IC challenges resulting from VN configurations. Finally in Section 5, a series of conclusions are drawn, which incorporate an outlook on bargaining concepts as part of our further work.

2 Basics

The quantification of VNs requires two fundamental considerations: First, the representation of VNs needs to be adapted to the needs of quantified analysis, which entails the formation of Value Network Dependency Models (cf. Section 2.1). Second, the market forces acting on individual firms are used as starting point for describing positioning of firms in VNs (cf. Section 2.2).

2.1 Value Network Dependency Models

In literature, e.g. [11], Value Models are known for modelling business relationships with defined interfaces for exchanging goods with economic partners, i.e. a mechanism for visually modelling Value Networks [11] such as e3Value [12]. An extension of e3Value named c3Value [13] introduces the goal modelling technique from [14] and Porter's strategic competition analysis [15] to e3Value. In contrast to e3Value, it applies a resource-centric representation targeting the dimensions of customers, capabilities, and competition through strategic resources modelling [11]. These dimensions are still modelled qualitatively in c3Value in order to maintain the fundamentals of e3Value (cf. [13]), which still leaves bargaining powers without quantified evidence.

---

[1] Verna Allee: `http://www.valuenetworksandcollaboration.com/`, last accessed: May 27, 2011.

Countervailing the absence of quantifications, we extend Value Models as VN representations by assigning costs, resource values, and cardinalities to relationships, in order to establish a so called Value Network Dependency Model (*VNDM*). Remember that cardinalities—as indicator for internal rivalry—define the number of instances being addressed by one relationship, e.g. an Information Service Provider (*InfSP*) can make business with a multitude of ECs. Similar to [11], a differentiation in resource types (values) transferred via relationships is applied in order to capture their economic influence on the VN. For simplicity reasons, the following five fundamental resource types are used: money, uncustomised exchangeable goods (ownership is linked to exchange), customised exchangeable goods, promises/requests/treaties (indirect ownership exchange), and intangible goods.

Such *VNDMs* consequently form the basis for the quantification of VNs through a dependency analysis (cf. Section 3). Explicitly, the quantified relationships of actor entities, e.g. Information Service Provider (*InfSP*), serve as starting point for calculating forces on firms within a VN (cf. Section 2.2). For our analysis, we have chosen an intermediary abstraction level—a differentiation which is very common in Model Driven Engineering, e.g. [16]—which enables the differentiation of Edge NSPs providing their services to InfSPs from those serving the end customers (*EC*). As a result of the non-linear value streams of the access and the service provisioning, traditional value chains cannot capture this example.

Figure 1 depicts an IC example with an *EC* who pays for a service requested from an *InfSP*. The service provisioning through the network is established by the Edge NSPs—providing access to the Internet—of the InfSP and the EC, as well as by the Transit NSPs connecting Edge NSPs. Both InfSP and EC have already paid (value φ) for their Internet access (solid line) exposing certain costs

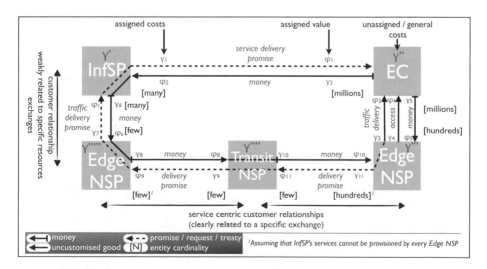

Fig. 1. The Interconnection market as Value Network Dependency Model

γ for the realisation of this access on the Edge NSPs. The EdgeNSPs in turn have to compensate the IC efforts from Transit NSP. Complementary, all actors have to face certain role-dependent costs for their participating in this VN, e.g. networking equipment by the EC, network investments by NSPs, or content production costs by the InfSP.

2.2   Porter's Five Forces

Porter's Five Forces on firms—industry rivalry, (bargaining) power of suppliers and customers, substitutes, and threats of new market entrants [10]—originate from a single-enterprise perspective, which stands in contrast to VNs' external view. Though, the concepts such as suppliers or customers can also be linked to directional relationships being used within VNs. Each relationship from a source actor to a target actor forms a supplier-customers relationship. The substitutes, e.g. switching from Transit NSPs to Content Delivery Network (*CDN*) providers, may be modelled by the effort for reshaping the VN. On the contrary, market entries may be quantified as costs (investments) for establishing the entrance of one specific entity instance.

The concept of industry rivalry cannot be directly linked to *VNDMs*, as competition instances of actors are not captured in VNs. Thus, this force is only implicitly targeted by inspecting the cardinalities and their effects on the dependencies of actors. Conceptually, cardinalities can indicate how many entity instances are available for taking on the role of this entity.

3   Entity Dependencies Δ^e

Let E be the set of all entities acting in a VN. By analysing a given *VNDM*—such as depicted in Figure 1—the dependencies of those entities on the VN are quantified by defining six relative *dependency indicators* calculated from properties of VN's relationships. Thus, by reinterpreting the threats firms have to face a quantified dependency concept is derived. The worth of an entity / entity instance for the VN is related to its dependency on the VN, i.e. the higher the total dependency of an entity on the VN, the higher is the likeliness of replacing it. The six (normalised) dependency indicators δ_i^e ($i = 1, \ldots, 6$; $e \in E$; cf. Figure 1) are aggregated to a single dependency indicator Δ^e as follows:

$$\Delta^e = \sum_{i=1}^{6} w_i * \delta_i^e \tag{1}$$

with weighting factors ($w_i \in [0,1]$) for each dependency indicator δ_i^e, and $\sum w_i = 1$. Five of the six dependencies indicators δ_i^e are constructed from Porter's well-known five forces on single firms. The sixth dependency indicator is constructed from the investigation on dependency effects resulting from the usage of different resource types (similar to the differentiation of [11]). Each dependency indicator δ_i^e takes a value in $[0,1]$ based on the analysis of its relationships R^e ($R^{e,in}$ for incoming, and $R^{e,out}$ for outgoing ones), as shown in the following:

1. **Dependency from Bargaining Power of Suppliers:** The bargaining power of suppliers (demanded resources) is calculated by analysing the value distribution of requested resources to particular entities. This is calculated as follows:

   The value φ of a single incoming relationship $r \in R^{e,in}$ to entity e is denoted by $\varphi(r)$. The bargaining powers can then be measured by analysing the value distributions of relationships, e.g. on the basis of information entropy [17], as indicator for disorders in systems. In this paper, however we reinterpret the efficiently calculable Gini coefficient—as metric for information impurity in information theory [18] (derived from the classical income distribution inequality calculation)—to a metric for value distributions among relationships. For this purpose, we define $p_r^{e,in}$ as fraction between the value φ of one incoming relationship $r \in R^{e,in}$ and the sum of values from all relationships of entity e. Note that the larger $p_r^{e,in}$, the more dependent is the entity on a single other entity in the VN. For *VNDMs*, this forms the a-priori probability of one single consumed value unit being dedicated to a specific relationship. Finally, an appropriate dependency indicator δ_i^e is calculated in respect to the maximum impurity in the VN based on the set of entities E and their incoming relationships R^{in} (a subset of all relationships of R of the VN).

$$p_r^{e,in} := \frac{\varphi(r)}{\sum\limits_{k \in R^{e,in}} \varphi(k)} \tag{2}$$

$$gini(R^{e,in}) := \sum\limits_{r \in R^{e,in}} (p_r^{e,in})^2 \tag{3}$$

$$\delta_1^e := \frac{gini(R^{e,in})}{\max\limits_{j \in E}\{gini(R^{j,in})\}} \tag{4}$$

   where $e \in E; r \in R^{e,in} \subseteq R^e \subset R$, and $gini(R^{e,in}) \leq 1$

   The resulting δ_1^e is also orthogonally related to the dependency δ_5^e, which however focuses on the replaceability of individual entity instances.

2. **Dependency from Bargaining Power of Customers:** The bargaining power of customers (to whom resources are sold) can be represented by the analysis of value distributions of provided resources to other entities. The customer-side bargaining dependency δ_2^e thus is calculated exactly like δ_1^e, where $R^{e,in}$ is replaced by $R^{e,out}$ and $R^{j,in}$ is replaced by $R^{j,out}$.

3. **Dependency from Substitutes** of the resources provided by entity e: For the value creation in VNs, a series of resources are required. By investments in technological developments or by utilising existing substitutes, each resource may be substituted by another one, e.g. in some cases IC may be replaced by CDN assistance. The required efforts for substituting resources are transferred to a VN-related dependency.

The lower the technical uniqueness and complexity of actor entity e's resources, the lower the difficulty of technically substituting e in the VN. Hence, the dependency of actor entities is related to the technical uniqueness of their goods being consumed via relationships (outgoing relationships $R^{e,out}$ of e). The substitution costs/efforts for a single produced activity/resource associated with one outward-pointing relationship r is denoted by $c_s(r)$. The sum of all costs for substituting entity e are $C_s(e)$.

$$C_s(e) := \sum_{r \in R^{e,out}} (c_s(r) * p_r^{e,out})$$

$$\delta_3^e := \begin{cases} 1 - \dfrac{C_s(e)}{\max\limits_{j \in E}\{C_s(j)\}}, & if \max\limits_{j \in E}\{C_s(j)\} \neq 0 \\ 1, & otherwise \end{cases} \tag{5}$$

4. **Dependency from Potential Entrants** in the market (substitution of an instance): The entrance in the market is modelled as cost for substituting the progress of producing the resources provided by an instance of an entity. The higher the costs c_m for replacing an instance of actor entity e (i.e. the instance substitution cost $c_m(e)$), the higher the probability of substitution (cf. Equation 6). Hence, the dependency of actor entities on the VN is related to the costs of instance substitution $c_m(e)$, e.g. costs for starting your own business for e's activities.

$$\delta_4^e := \begin{cases} 1 - \dfrac{c_m(e)}{\max\limits_{j \in E}\{c_m(j)\}}, & if \max\limits_{j \in E}\{c_m(j)\} \neq 0 \\ 1, & otherwise \end{cases} \tag{6}$$

5. **Dependency from Industry Rivalry:** The concept of industry rivalry cannot be directly linked to *VNDMs*, as competition of one actor role is not captured in VNs. Thus, a dependency related to high industry competition is implicitly addressed by analysing the cardinality values. Cardinalities can indicate how many entity instances are available for overtaking the role of one entity. In particular, the more entity instances can play the same role, the higher is the dependency of a single instance on the VN, and the less is their power in a bargaining process. Another implicit indicator for rivalry is given by profit levels of entities being subject to margins resulting from competition on the market.

A relationship pointing from entity e to another entity holds a source-side cardinality s (i.e. the upper-bound instances of e) and a target-side cardinality t (i.e. the potential business partners for e through r)—cf. Figure 2. The higher the cardinality s for r, the higher is the dependency of an instance of e on the VN. Contrary, the lower the upper bound cardinality t of relationship r, the lower the dependency on the VN. Obviously, those two views on cardinalities are systemwide dependent on each other, thus one is eliminated—by choice only the referred entities' cardinalities is viewed at. Formally, this dependency indicator is expressed with δ_5^e (cf. Equation 8). The weight p_r^e

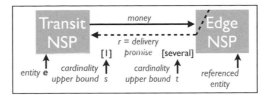

Fig. 2. The cardinalities for a relationship of entity e

is defined in analogy to $p_r^{e,in}$ (see Equation 2), but refers to all relationship values independently of their direction. Thus it eliminates a bias from value specific differences of the relationships of entity e (cf. Equation 2).

$$\mathcal{C}_t(e) = \sum_{r \in R^e} (card_t(r) * p_r^e), \qquad card_t(r) > 0 \qquad (7)$$

$$\delta_5^e = 1 - \frac{\mathcal{C}_t(e)}{\max_{j \in E}\{\mathcal{C}_t(j)\}} \qquad (8)$$

6. **Resource Type Dependency:** The flexibility of resource types in selling them to different actor entities (instances), corresponds to the dependency of actors on the VN involving their market dynamics. For example, monetary goods are more flexible than produced goods or even specifically customised or intangible goods. The type dependency *type(i)* takes a value between *0* and *1* where *1* represents the maximum resource type dependency on the VN, i.e. it can only be used for this specific purpose.

$$\mathcal{T}(e) := \sum_{r \in R_{out}^e} (type(i) * p_r^e) \le 1$$

$$\delta_6^e := \begin{cases} \frac{\mathcal{T}(e)}{\max_{j \in E}\{\mathcal{T}(j)\}}, & if \max_{j \in E}\{\mathcal{T}(j)\} \ne 0 \\ 0, & otherwise \end{cases} \qquad (9)$$

In Equation 9, an average dependency value is calculated from the type dependency of each relationship r of each entity $e \in E$.

4   Case Study: Interconnection Dependencies

In this section, the previously introduced theoretical concepts are used for analysing the role of Transit NSPs in a typical IC VN (cf. Figure 1). Exemplarily, *Video on Demand* (VoD) streaming of one movie (price of *$10*) from a server in *New York* to an end customer in *London* is quantitatively modelled (cf. Figure 3). By the quantification of entity dependencies, the ability to replace Transit NSPs is investigated. The dependencies δ_i^e may be weighted by individually adjusting w_i, but for reasons of simplicity we assume that $w_i = 1/6$ for all $i = 1, \ldots, 6$. The individual dependencies are calculated as follows:

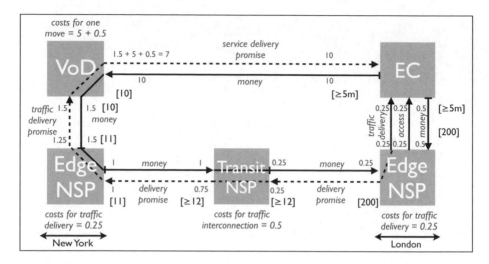

Fig. 3. The Value Network Dependency Model of a Video on Demand scenario

Supply (δ_1^e) / Customers (δ_2^e). The values depicted in Figure 3 are assumptions based on a series of market indicators. These quantifications have been adjusted and uniformed to the process of selling one single movie to one single EC, where all costs are assumed to be completely and truthfully assigned. Based on the analysis of market offers[2], we set the movie rental price to *$10* for offering a single HD movie of cinema-quality with assured quality high-speed IC. *$5* of the movie price are used for compensating the initial efforts for the copyright holders. Furthermore, we dedicate *$0.5* to the platform costs, i.e. stream processing, billing, marketing, etc. *$1.5* is paid to the chained NSPs, where Edge NSPs are assumed to have costs of *$0.25* and the Transit NSP of *$0.5* (with lower margins[3]). In contrast to all other entities, the Edge NSP of the EC is paid from two sides: the delivery to the EC is paid by the EC (access contract), whereas the assured quality IC is paid via the InfSP chain of transfers, where this entity receives *$0.25* as compensation.

Rivalry (δ_5^e). Due to the high quality and traffic volume requirements, we assume that VoD platforms require one of the *11* US providers with more than one million customers[4] (multihoming is not modelled in this calculation). The EC

---

[2] Itunes Movie: www.itunes.com; Amazon Unbox: http://www.amazon.com/b/? &node=16261631; CinemaNow: http://www.cinemanow.com/; Blockbuster: http:// www.blockbuster.com/download; etc., last accessed: May 27 2011.

[3] Sharply falling transit cost curves, which indicate high competition and/or high technical improvements. Original source http://drpeering.net/white-papers/ Internet-Transit-Pricing-Historical-And-Projected.php

[4] Jupiter Research taken from http://www.isp-planet.com/research/rankings/ usa.html, last accessed: May 27 2011.

can choose from *200* providers available in London[5]. There exist at least *12* recognised Tier-1 providers providing Transit IC. Popular on-demand offers like BBC's iPlayer[6] with million of customers indicate a huge potential in the UK— even up to 150 million VoD users worldwide could be realistic [7]. For paid services per cinema-quality movie, the potential may be lower[8]. Regional offers in the UK as well as some international platforms, trigger our assumption that the same content may be accessed from *10* different platforms from the UK.

Substitutes (δ_3^e).   The efforts for substituting Edge NSPs are very high, as replacements for fixed-line / wireless broadband connections to every household are required. Transit NSPs may be replaced by Peering agreements between the VoD platform and the Edge NSPs or between the Edge NSPs. Full substitution by Edge NSPs costs $11 * 200 * 10000$ [9], whereas it is $10 * 200 * 10000$ for VoD providers. The multipliers 10 and 11 respectively are subject to the cardinalities of these entities. Alternatively, CDNs—whose prices are rumoured to be much lower than for Transit[10]—can substitute Transit IC in this scenario. VoD provider platforms may be substituted by an alternation of distribution channels, e.g. through classical cable-TV based offers or traditional video rental. Due to the absence of concrete and aligned numbers, we thus take the following substitution dependencies: end customers = 0, Edge NSP = 0.33, VoD provider = 0.33, and Transit NSP = 1.

Potential Entrance (δ_4^e).   The efforts in establishing/replacing Edge NSPs' networks are very high[11]. Virtual networks are still subject to the pricing schemes of existing NSPs. To become a Tier-1 Transit NSP (cf. network architecture in [19]) entails a globally recognised market position (billions of investments) allowing free IC with all other Tier-1 NSPs. Replacing a VoD provider serving the same movie, is technical less effortful, but encompasses legal and brand-related challenges. First, the contracts with content producers have to be signed. The

---

[5] We assume that 200 of 400 are able to deliver such a service in the London. Original source: http://www.nationmaster.com/graph/int_int_ser_pro-internet-service-providers, last accessed: May 27 2011

[6] FrequencyCast: http://www.frequencycast.co.uk/ondemand.html, last accessed: May 27 2011

[7] Metrics 2.0: http://www.metrics2.com/blog/2006/09/04/videoondemand_to_reach_13_billion_by_2010_with_150.html, last accessed: May 27 2011

[8] We assume around 1 million interested customers.

[9] In 2011, public Peering costs per connection were $10 000; Source: http://drpeering.net/white-papers/Internet-Transit-Pricing-Historical-And-Projected.php, last accessed: May 27 2011

[10] $0.025 per downloaded GB in 2010, Original source: http://drpeering.net/AskDrPeering/blog/articles/Peering_vs_Transit___The_Business_Case_for_Peering.html, last accessed: May 27 2011

[11] Derived from Fiber-to-the-Home effort analysis by the ICT Regulation Toolkit: http://www.ictregulationtoolkit.org/en/PracticeNote.aspx?id=2974, last accessed: May 27 2011

difficulty is reflected by great global and local offer variations. Second, the estimated values of competing brands like Apple are high—$57.4 billion dollars in 2010^{12}. Thus, the effort for compensating a brand may be highest, but offers by globally established companies are realistic. In contrast, EC's may be recruited by several dollars effort. We assume following dependencies: Edge NSPs = 0.33, Transit NSP = 0.33, VoD provider = 0.66, and EC = 1.

Resource Types (δ_6^e). The resource types of *VNDMs* are weighted as follows: Money = 0 (money is most flexible), uncustomised resource = 0.33, and promises / requests / treaties and customised goods = 0.66 (needs to be signed, and is therefore more specific).

Table 1. Dependencies in the VoD scenario on basis of one streamed video

	VoD	EC	Edge NSP (VoD)	Edge NSP (EC)	Transit NSP
δ_1^e	0.85187	1	0.57294	0.61212	0.74923
δ_2^e	0.85028	1	0.57187	0.36658	0.74783
δ_3^e	0.33	0	0.33	0.33	1
δ_4^e	0.66	1	0.33	0.33	0.33
δ_5^e	0	0.99998	0.99999	0.23333	0.99994
δ_6^e	1	0.65079	0.26667	0.11111	0.13333
Δ^e	0.44869	**0.66666**	**0.46747**	**0.31201**	**0.63783**

The results of Table 1 reveal a high overall dependency on the VN by ECs, closely followed by Transit NSPs. Medium dependency levels are observed for VoD providers, and Edge NSPs connected to the VoD provider. The lowest dependencies are achieved by Edge NSPs being connected to a multitude of ECs. This may be reflected in endeavours of Transit NSPs to remodel their role in the Value Network, e.g. by market mechanisms with modified revenue streams [20]. On the other hand, the higher the power of VoD providers (the opposite of the dependency on the VN) implies for this scenario that the power for shaping the VN is held by VoD providers. This is supported by theories which discuss the flattening of Internet hierarchies triggered by InfSPs [21].

These results also indicate competitive advantages for global NSPs acting in both roles (at VoD- and at EC-side)—aggregated to *0.389*. One entity providing all network services may be still beneficial (*0.4724*) to avoid an InfSP-side VN remodelling. Thus, it is very likely an attractive option to eliminate the Transit NSPs role for InfSPs and other NSPs.

---

[12] Forbes: http://www.forbes.com/2010/07/28/apple-google-microsoft-ibm-nike-disney-bmw-forbes-cmo-network-most-valuable-brands.html, last accessed: May 27 2011.

5   Conclusions

In literature, the analysis of Value Networks (VNs), e.g. [4], is largely discussed on a conceptual and qualitative level. In this paper, we have proposed a concept for quantifying the dependencies of actor entities on the VN through a series of dependency indicators, i.e. indicators from the (Bargaining) Power of Suppliers, (Bargaining) Power of Customers, Substitutes, Potential Entrants, Industry Rivalry, and Resource Types. These indicators have been derived from well-known concepts in literatures, e.g. Porter's Five Forces, forming a linkage of classical structural determinants of market competition and attractiveness with complex and non-linear VNs. For enabling the quantification of VNs, visual representations such as Value Models have been evolved to Value Network Dependency Models (*VNDMs*) modelling costs, values, and cardinalities of relationships and entities respectively. By applying our concept in a case study on Video on Demand we could argue that the role of Transit NSPs is very attractive to be re-modelled or eliminated. These results have been subject to a set of assumptions, which are intended to be replaced by market information in future analysis. The requirement of such information can be regarded as notable disadvantage for the proposed method in practice, which may be outweighed by the expressiveness of quantified results. Moreover, we intend to evaluate our technique with an empirical study based on historic evolvements of more complex VNs.

With our dependency indicators we also anticipate the formation of a bargaining mechanism for VNs, which extends the concept of Shapley values [22]. By defining a VN as grand coalition of all entities, a payout to each entity may be defined by opposing actual achieved profits per entity/instance to their dependency on the VN. Hence, such a mechanism may be used for calculating the worth of an entity instance for the VN, i.e. the lower the dependency of one entity on the VN, the higher the dependency on the VN on the instances of this entity.

References

1. Porter, M.E.: Competitive Advantage: Creating and Sustaining Superior Performance. Free Press (1985)
2. Hakansson, H., Snehota, I.: No Business is an Island: The Network Concept of Business Strategy. Scandinavian Journal of Management, 187–200 (1989)
3. Normann, R., Ramirez, R.: Designing Interactive Strategy: From the Value Chain to the Value Constellation. John Wiley & Sons, Chichester (1994)
4. Gulati, R., Nohria, N., Zaheer, A.: Strategic Networks. Strategic Management Journal 21, 203–215 (2000)
5. Gulati, R., Lavie, D., Singh, H.: The Nature of Partnering Experience and the Gains from Alliances. Strategic Management Journal 30(11), 1213–1233 (2009)
6. Timmers, P.: Business Models for Electronic Commerce. Electronic Markets 8(2) (1998)
7. Teece, D.J.: Business Models, Business Strategy and Innovation. Long Range Planning 43(2–3), 172–194 (2010)

8. Allee, V., Schwabe, O.: Value Networks and the True Nature of Collaboration. Digitial edition edn. ValueNetworks, LLC (2011)

9. Allee, V.: Value Network Analysis and Value Conversion of Tangible and Intangible Assets. Emerald Journal of Intellectual Capital 9(1), 5–24 (2008)

10. Porter, M.E.: How Competitive Forces Shape Strategy. Harvard Business Review 102 (1979)

11. Biem, A., Caswell, N.: A Value Network Model for Strategic Analysis. In: Proceedings of the 41st Annual Hawaii International Conference on System Sciences, pp. 361–367 (2008)

12. Gordijn, J., Akkermans, H.: E3-value: Design and Evaluation of e-Business Models. IEEE Intelligent Systems 16(4), 11–17 (2001)

13. Weigand, H., Johannesson, P., Andersson, B., Bergholtz, M., Edirisuriya, A., Ilayperuma, T.: Strategic Analysis Using Value Modeling–The c3-Value Approach. In: Proceedings of the 40th Annual Hawaii International Conference on System Sciences, HICSS 2007, vol. 40. IEEE, Los Alamitos (2007)

14. Yu, E.: Modelling Strategic Relationships for Process Reengineering. PhD thesis, University of Toronto, Dept. of Computer Science (1995)

15. Porter, M.: Competitive Strategy: Techniques for Analyzing Industries and Competitors: with a new Introduction. Free Press (1980)

16. Jouault, F., Kurtev, I.: On the Architectural Alignment of ATL and QVT. In: Proceedings of the 2006 ACM Symposium on Applied Computing, pp. 1188–1195. ACM, New York (2006)

17. Shannon, C.E.: A Mathematical Theory of Communication. ACM SIGMOBILE Mobile Computing and Communications Review 5(1), 3–5 (2001)

18. Breiman, L., Friedman, J.H., Stone, C.A., Olshen, R.A.: Classification and Regression Trees, 1st edn. Chapman and Hall, Boca Raton (1984)

19. Kurose, J., Ross, K.: Computer Networking: A Top Down Approach. Addison-Wesley, Reading (2008)

20. Valancius, V., Feamster, N., Johari, R., Vazirani, V.: MINT: a Market for INternet Transit. In: Proceedings of the 2008 ACM CoNEXT Conference. ACM, New York (2008)

21. Gill, P., Arlitt, M., Li, Z., Mahanti, A.: The Flattening Internet Topology: Natural Evolution, Unsightly Barnacles or Contrived Collapse? In: Claypool, M., Uhlig, S. (eds.) PAM 2008. LNCS, vol. 4979, pp. 1–10. Springer, Heidelberg (2008)

22. Shapley, L.S.: Value for n-Person Games. In: Contributions to the Theory of Games. Annals of Mathematical Studies v.28, vol. 2, pp. 307–317. Princeton University Press, Princeton (1953)

Author Index